FOOD FESTIVALS
of Northern California

TRAVELER'S GUIDE
AND
COOKBOOK

Bob Carter

FALCON™
Helena, Montana

($20. on Amazon)

© 1997 Bob Carter

Illustrations © 1997 Peter Grosshauser

Published by Falcon Press® Publishing Co., Inc.
Helena and Billings, Montana

Design, typesetting, and other prepress work by Falcon Press®, Helena, Montana.

Printed in Canada.

Library of Congress Cataloging-in-Publicaion Data

Carter, Bob, 1932-
    Food festivals of Northern California : traveler's guide and
cookbook / Bob Carter.
        p.   cm.
    Includes index.
    ISBN 1-56044-527-0
    1. Cookery, American—California style.   2. Festivals—California,
Northern—Guidebooks.   I. Title.
TX715.2.C34C384 1997
641.59794—dc21   96-40514
                                                   CIP

CONTENTS

ACKNOWLEDGMENTS V

INTRODUCTION VI

USING THIS BOOK VII

LOCATOR MAP IX

THE FESTIVALS:

1. A La Carte, Marin County 1

2. A La Carte, A La Park, San Francisco 5

3. Abalone Festival, Mendocino 9

4. Apricot Fiesta, Patterson 14

5. Art a La Carte, Mammoth Lakes 19

6. Art & Pumpkin Festival, Half Moon Bay 24

7. Asparagus Festival, Stockton 28

8. Autumn Food & Wine Jubilee, Squaw Valley 33

9. Blackberry Festival, Lake County 37

10. Cherry Blossom Festival, Lodi 41

11. Chili Cook-Off, Willow Creek 46

12. Chocolate Festival, Oakdale 50

13. Clam Chowder Cook-Off, Santa Cruz 55

14. Coastal Christmas, Humboldt County 59

15. Dry Bean Festival, Tracy 64

16. Eggplant Festival, Loomis 69

17. Festa Italiana, Sacramento 74

18. Festival of Goat Cheese & North Coast Wine, Sonoma County ... 78

19. Fish Feed & Art Festival, Trinidad 82

20. Garlic Festival, Gilroy 86

21. Grape Stomp, Murphys 91

22. Grecian Festival, Novato 96

CONTENTS

23. Historic Christmas Bed & Breakfast Tour, Calaveras County ... 100

24. Italian Festa, Oakland 107

25. Lambtown, U.S.A. Festival, Dixon 112

26. Mid-Summer Scandinavian Festival, Ferndale 115

27. Mountain Harvest Festival/A Taste of Quincy, Quincy 120

28. Mushroom Mardi Gras, Morgan Hill 124

29. Mustard Festival, Napa Valley 128

30. Onion Festival, Vacaville 134

31. Oyster Festival, Arcata 138

32. Pear Fair, Courtland 143

33. Pear Festival, Kelseyville 148

34. Prune Festival, Yuba City 153

35. Pumpkin-Fest, Healdsburg 157

36. Salmon Festival, Klamath 162

37. Seafood, Art & Wine Festival, Bodega Bay 167

38. Snowfest!, Lake Tahoe 171

39. Solar Cook-Off, Taylorsville 176

40. Timberfest, Sierra County 182

41. Walnut Festival, Walnut Creek 187

42. Whale Festival, Fort Bragg 192

43. Zucchini Festival, Angels Camp 196

APPENDIX A: FURTHER FEASTINGS 201

APPENDIX B: CERTIFIED FARMERS' MARKETS 204

APPENDIX C: INFORMATION DIRECTORY 206

RECIPE AND CATEGORY INDEX 209

ABOUT THE AUTHOR 214

"I like this place, and willingly would waste my time in it."

Shakespeare, *As You Like It* and motto of the Renaissance Pleasure Faire

ACKNOWLEDGMENTS

I owe my personal thanks to dozens of fellow travelers, festival organizers, residents, chefs, cooks, and food lovers for sharing their superlative recipes and treasured support with me.

Two people deserve special mention. I'm indebted to computer whiz Terry Poland for his technical advice, unlimited patience, and critical guidance throughout this endeavor. Cookbook author and food consultant Gail Hobbs made suggestions and contributed pointers that helped me immeasurably. Without their valuable contributions this book would not have been possible nor would it have seen the light of day.

The following agencies provided a wealth of information, advice, and encouragement.

American Dairy Goat Products Association
California Apple Commission
California Avocado Commission
California Date Administrative Committee
California Dry Bean Advisory Board
California Fig Advisory Board
California Office of Tourism
California Olive Industry
California Pear Advisory Board
California Pistachio Commission
California Raisin Advisory Board
California Seafood Council
California Strawberry Advisory Board

Cherry Marketing Institute
Maine Lobster Promotion Council
Mushroom Council
National Coffee Association of U.S.A.
National Fisheries Institute
National Oyster Cook-off
Northwest Cherry Growers
Oak Glen Applegrowers Association
Sunkist Growers
U.S.A. Rice Council
Walnut Marketing Board
Wine Institute

INTRODUCTION

When I was growing up in a small California community, local celebrations were looked upon as exciting opportunities to eat sensational food, savor lively entertainment, and be as spirited as the law allowed. Californians love to have a good time. Give us an excuse, and we'll organize a noteworthy event and invite the world to attend.

Every year tens of thousands of California residents and visitors attend one or more of the state's eclectic array of food-oriented festivals and culinary celebrations. From the smallest of rural communities to the sophistication and diversity of large urban areas, hundreds of fun-for-all, hometown events take place every season of the year. California's varied festivals provide enjoyable family-style entertainment, gourmet restaurant samplings, and some of the best homemade tastes found anywhere. It's not a bad idea to plan to attend them all!

When I sat down to write this book, I had several goals in mind. I wanted to acknowledge the vital contribution California's agriculture makes to the world's food supply. I desired to highlight a wide variety of communities—large and small—and extol the diversity of their residents. Mainly, I yearned to share my overwhelming desire to experience the excitement of travel, food, and entertainment. But most of all, I hoped to inspire my readers to experience the joy of celebrating life to its fullest. I hope you'll let me know if I succeeded.

If I missed your favorite festival, or you want to contact me, I'd love to hear from you. Write me in care of *Falcon Press Publishing Company, Inc.,* P.O. Box 1718, Helena, MT 59624.

If you're so inclined, plan your traveling schedule to include one or more of my favorite events. If you do, you'll probably see me there, sampling some of the most extraordinary experiences California has to offer.

Happy trails and bon appétit!

USING THIS BOOK

For many travelers, attending a local festival or celebration helps make a trip more memorable. To avoid disappointment, it is advised you verify event dates, times, fees, and activities in advance.

Although some of the recipes have been adapted slightly for consistency in format, I've tried to allow each contributor's personality to shine through. Whenever you see a chef's hat, you'll obtain some insight into the recipe. When I've felt the need to add my bit of personal observation, you'll find it designated with a small writing pad and pen.

ORGANIZATION OF FESTIVALS: The events detailed in this book are arranged by festival name, followed by city or county location. No more than one festival for each location has been described in detail.

INFORMATION DIRECTORY: It is strongly suggested you write, call, or fax for additional information regarding destinations and events. The *Information Directory* portion of this guide includes contacts for individual festivals, chambers of commerce, and visitor bureaus. These agencies will provide you details regarding accommodations, dining, shopping, recreation, attractions, and additional special events and festivals.

FURTHER FEASTINGS: Since some communities hold several food-oriented events during the year, when available these additional events are listed in the *Further Feastings* section of this book.

FARMERS' MARKETS: California is well known for its agricultural variety and many food enthusiasts visit local farmers' markets on a regular basis. This book includes a guide to local markets. You may want to visit one or more during your travels. These markets vary widely in size and offerings. If you want more specifics about each, a local telephone number is provided. Due to seasonal produce availability, it's wise to confirm dates and times in advance.

CALIFORNIA CELEBRATIONS: Each year the California Trade and Commerce Agency publishes a small booklet listing special events and ethnic celebrations for California's 12 tourism regions. A complimentary copy of the guide to nearly 1,000 reasons to celebrate may be obtained by contacting the California Division of Tourism, *California Celebrations,* P.O. Box 1499, Sacramento, CA 95812.

SPECIAL NOTE: Although diligent efforts have been made to confirm the accuracy of information contained in this work, neither the publisher nor the author is responsible for errors or inaccuracies or for changes occurring after publication. Event offerings sometime change. To avoid disappointment, it's strongly suggested, once again, that festival date, fee, location, and specific activities be confirmed in advance.

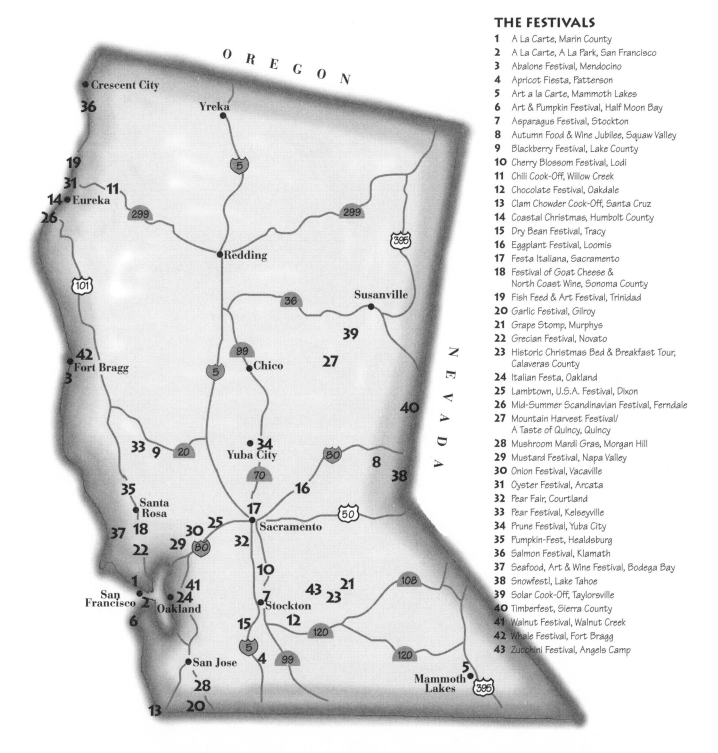

O R E G O N

Crescent City

Yreka

36

19

31 11

14 Eureka

26

299

299

395

Redding

Susanville

36

39

27

42 Fort Bragg

3

99

5 Chico

40

33 9

20

34

Yuba City

80

35

Santa Rosa

70

8

38

37 18

25

30

16

22

29 80

32

17 Sacramento

50

1

41

10

San Francisco

2

24 Oakland

7 Stockton

43 23 21

108

6

12

15

San Jose

120

28

5

4 99

120

5

20

Mammoth Lakes

13

395

N E V A D A

101

THE FESTIVALS

1 A La Carte, Marin County
2 A La Carte, A La Park, San Francisco
3 Abalone Festival, Mendocino
4 Apricot Fiesta, Patterson
5 Art a la Carte, Mammoth Lakes
6 Art & Pumpkin Festival, Half Moon Bay
7 Asparagus Festival, Stockton
8 Autumn Food & Wine Jubilee, Squaw Valley
9 Blackberry Festival, Lake County
10 Cherry Blossom Festival, Lodi
11 Chili Cook-Off, Willow Creek
12 Chocolate Festival, Oakdale
13 Clam Chowder Cook-Off, Santa Cruz
14 Coastal Christmas, Humbolt County
15 Dry Bean Festival, Tracy
16 Eggplant Festival, Loomis
17 Festa Italiana, Sacramento
18 Festival of Goat Cheese &
   North Coast Wine, Sonoma County
19 Fish Feed & Art Festival, Trinidad
20 Garlic Festival, Gilroy
21 Grape Stomp, Murphys
22 Grecian Festival, Novato
23 Historic Christmas Bed & Breakfast Tour,
   Calaveras County
24 Italian Festa, Oakland
25 Lambtown, U.S.A. Festival, Dixon
26 Mid-Summer Scandinavian Festival, Ferndale
27 Mountain Harvest Festival/
   A Taste of Quincy, Quincy
28 Mushroom Mardi Gras, Morgan Hill
29 Mustard Festival, Napa Valley
30 Onion Festival, Vacaville
31 Oyster Festival, Arcata
32 Pear Fair, Courtland
33 Pear Festival, Kelseyville
34 Prune Festival, Yuba City
35 Pumpkin-Fest, Healdsburg
36 Salmon Festival, Klamath
37 Seafood, Art & Wine Festival, Bodega Bay
38 Snowfest!, Lake Tahoe
39 Solar Cook-Off, Taylorsville
40 Timberfest, Sierra County
41 Walnut Festival, Walnut Creek
42 Whale Festival, Fort Bragg
43 Zucchini Festival, Angels Camp

A LA CARTE
MARIN COUNTY
Annual. Memorial Day weekend.

The Marin A La Carte celebration is held in the city of San Rafael. It's an opportunity to sample the cuisine from Marin and Sonoma county restaurants, check out cooking demonstrations by top area chefs, enjoy the excellence of California premium varietals, experiment with the world of microbreweries, browse through a fine arts show, or just sit on the grass and enjoy the continuous entertainment. What more could you ask?

You'll soon discover that the irrestistible samplings are not only hearty, some include the entire menu from several top-rated restaurants. Top entertainment is provided by noted musical talents, and artwork by eighty select artisans is displayed and sold.

Feel free to bring the entire family to this benefit for the Marin Ballet, Marin Opera, Marin Symphony, and Youth in Arts. An extensive children's area includes cooking experiences for youngsters, face painting, mural drawing, hat creating, paper folding, and other diversions for the wee bunch. The kids are in good hands in their special area organized by Youth in Arts.

After you've tasted, be sure to stop by the souvenir booth to vote for your favorite restaurant. The winning restaurant receives the Best of Marin A la Carte award.

Marin A La Carte is held in San Rafael's 20-acre Civic Center Lagoon Park located off U.S. Highway 101.

COQ AU VIN
Classic Chicken Casserole

1 free-range chicken cut into
8 pieces

1 onion, peeled, sliced

2 carrots, peeled, cut in batonnets
or fine rounds

2 bottles red Burgundy wine

1 tablespoon olive oil

2 cloves garlic, minced

1 or 2 bay leaves

1 sprig thyme

1 tablespoon black peppercorns

salt and pepper to taste

4 tablespoons vegetable oil

2 cups veal or chicken stock

1/2 pound butter

1/2 slab of bacon, blanched,
cut in pieces

24 pearl onions, peeled, blanched

1/2 pound button mushrooms,
cleaned

1 bunch parsley, chopped

Marinate the chicken, onion, and carrots in red wine, olive oil, garlic, bay leaf, thyme, and peppercorns. Cover, then refrigerate overnight.

The next day, remove the chicken and vegetables from the marinade. Drain and pat dry. Strain the marinade through a fine chinois or sieve. Reserve.

Season chicken with salt and pepper on both sides. In a large skillet, heat the vegetable oil. Add the chicken, a few pieces at a time, starting with the legs and thighs. Sauté until golden brown on all sides. Add onion and carrot mixture. Transfer to a dutch oven or a large oven-proof serving casserole.

Deglaze skillet with marinade, then transfer to the chicken casserole. Bring to a boil and add veal or chicken stock. Simmer for 1 1/2 hours.

Melt butter in skillet and add blanched bacon, pearl onions, and mushrooms. Sauté for a few minutes. Drain extra fat. A few minutes before chicken is ready, spoon vegetables onto a serving dish and sprinkle with fresh parsley. Top vegetables with chicken.

Chef Roland Passot
Left Bank & La Folie
Larkspur, CA

LASAGNA ALA FERRARESE

Melt butter, add flour, and pour hot milk into mixture. Cook until thick. Add salt and white pepper to taste. Set aside.

Sauté mixed ground meat; when browned, add red wine. Simmer until wine is reduced. Add carrot, onion, and celery. Let cook several minutes until vegetables soften. Add tomato purée, sage, rosemary, and garlic. Add enough water to cover the meat mixture and let the sauce simmer 2 to 3 hours. Add additional water, if needed, throughout the cooking process. Add salt and pepper to taste.

Place a single layer of cooked or fresh spinach lasagna-style pasta in a buttered baking tray. Cover with a layer of Parmesan cheese, meat sauce, and Béchamel sauce. Repeat the operation until all the mixtures are used. Finish with Parmesan cheese and bake in oven at 250° for 20 minutes or until brown.

Chef Edmundo Sarti
Il Foranio Restaurant & Bakery
Corte Madera, CA

 The spinach pasta for this lasagna with white sauce may be made from scratch or purchased already made.

Béchamel Sauce
1½ ounces butter

1 ounce flour

2½ cups hot milk

salt and white pepper

Meat Sauce
10 ounces mixed ground meat (pork, beef, and veal)

8 ounces red wine

½ cup chopped carrot

½ cup chopped onion

½ cup stalk of celery

2 tablespoons tomato purée

pinch of chopped sage, rosemary, and garlic

water

salt and pepper to taste

Parmesan cheese to taste

1 16-ounce package spinach pasta, dried or fresh

FOCACCIA MADE EASY

1/2 tablespoon sugar

2 1/2 cups warm water

3/4 tablespoon active dry yeast

3/4 cup olive oil

2 tablespoons salt

1 tablespoon rosemary

2 1/4 pounds flour

Combine sugar, water, and yeast. Set aside for yeast to activate (about 15 minutes). When yeast is ready, add oil, salt, and rosemary to the liquid and start incorporating the liquid into the flour to form dough. You can use a mixer or do it by hand. Do not overwork the dough.

When a well-mixed dough is ready, pat a little oil on top and cover with a wet towel. Set in a warm place to rise for 30 minutes. When risen, empty dough onto a flat baking pan. Spread out evenly by hand or use rolling pin. Handle dough gently. Let rise again for 90 minutes.

Bake in oven at 425° for 40 minutes or until golden brown.

Chef Sunita Dutt
Chinook Restaurant and Cafe
San Rafael, CA

 Various toppings for this dough include: caramelized onion, walnuts, goat cheese, Roma tomatoes and basil, green onions and sliced tomatoes.

A LA CARTE, A LA PARK

SAN FRANCISCO
Annual. Labor Day weekend.

When was the last time your heart skipped a beat? That's what happens when most visitors first lay eyes on the fabulous city by the bay. It's the skyline, bridges, and natural beauty that make San Francisco so very special.

San Francisco's premier festival of food, music, wine, and spirits features many of the city's most-noted restaurants and chefs, finest wines, and noted microbreweries. Sponsored by Absolut Vodka and a host of local cosponsors, the spirited festival takes place in Golden Gate Park.

Once inside A La Carte, A La Park, you'll wander from tent to colorful tent, sampling mouth-watering dishes and beverages while enjoying live entertainment that includes spicy Cajun zydeco, smooth blues, contemporary jazz, and more.

Bay area chefs pull out the stops and present their trademark dishes, plus give food demonstrations. Thus, you can take an incredible tastebud tour of San Francisco right at the festival site.

To complement the festival samplings and sounds, the Absolut Bistro offers cocktails and food in a garden setting with umbrella tables. The beer garden serves up ales, lagers, and porters from more than twenty California microbreweries. Throughout the festival, top wineries pour their best vintages, served in commemorative glasses.

San Francisco has long been known as one of California's food meccas. Here's your chance to savor some of the city's finest food, beverages, and music in a setting of natural beauty.

PAELLA VALENCIANA

Savory Seafood and Rice Dish

6 tablespoons olive oil

4 chicken breasts

2 red peppers, diced

2 green peppers, diced

1 yellow onion, diced

2 cloves garlic, chopped

2 tablespoons chopped shallots

1 tablespoon saffron threads or

1/2 teaspoon powdered saffron

1 cup white wine

1 pound chorizo

24 clams

8 crab legs

24 mussels

6 ounces scallops

8 ounces calamari

8 ounces prawns

8 ounces white fish

4 cups fish fumet or chicken stock

1 1/2 cups fresh-diced tomatoes

12-ounce can stewed tomatoes

3 cups rice

salt and pepper to taste

Garnish

1/4 cup green peas

1/4 cup diced scallions

1/4 cup diced red peppers

Heat olive oil in a large paella pan or frying pan, add the chicken and cook until golden brown. Add peppers, onion, garlic, and shallots; sauté for about 2 minutes. Add the saffron and wine, cook 1 minute. Add the chorizo and seafood and let cook for another 3 minutes. Add fumet or stock and let it steam the shellfish open for about 2 to 5 minutes more. Add your tomatoes and rice. Mix all ingredients well.

Cook in preheated 350° oven for about 20 minutes or until most of the juices have been absorbed. Remove from oven, fluff the rice, and arrange seafood on top in a decorative manner. Garnish with peas, scallions, and red peppers.

Chef Pachi Calvo-y-Perez
PJ's Oysterbed
San Francisco, CA

FRESH TUNA SALADE NIÇOISE

Heat oil and water until the water begins to sizzle, then turn the flame off. Add the sachet and poach tuna lightly to medium rare, should take about 4 minutes.

Purée anchovies with lemon juice, slowly drizzle in olive oil and emulsify. Set aside.

Assemble a salad of lettuce, beets, radishes, fava beans, haricot vert, and tomato wedges. Place tuna in center and top with a dollop of the anchlode.

Chef Melissa Kelly
Restaurant Lulu
San Francisco, CA

4 to 6 ounces yellowfin tuna medallions

olive oil (to poach tuna)

1 tablespoon water
(in the pot with oil)

Sachet
fresh thyme

whole black peppercorns

garlic cloves

bay leaves

Anchlode
20 anchovies

2 tablespoons lemon juice

1 cup olive oil

Salad
mache lettuce

chioga beets, blanched

radishes

fava beans

haricot vert

tomato wedges

FROMAGE BLANC WITH CARAMELIZED ONIONS AND SPICED CRACKERS

Cheese Mixture

1 tablespoon butter

1 large white onion,
peeled and sliced

1 teaspoon salt

8 ounces pitted prunes, sliced

3 ounces white wine

1 pound fromage blanc goat cheese,
softened

lemon juice

Crackers

1 cup wheat flour

2 cups all-purpose flour

2 pinches curry powder

1 pinch cayenne pepper

1 teaspoon dried thyme leaves

2 tablespoons chopped fennel fronds

1 teaspoon salt

2 tablespoons cold butter

1 cup cold water, more as needed

Melt butter in heavy saucepan or skillet, add onions and salt, cook over low heat 5 to 7 minutes. Add prunes, continue until onions are very soft and translucent. Add wine, reduce uncovered until dry. Combine onion mixture with goat cheese and season with lemon juice to taste.

To prepare crackers: Preheat oven to 400°. Mix flours, spices, herbs, and salt. Add butter in pieces and cut in with fingers or a fork until it resembles a coarse meal. Add water and knead until dough is smooth. Refrigerate for 30 minutes before rolling. Roll dough to $1/8$-inch thickness, prick with a fork. Cut to desired shape. Bake on an ungreased baking sheet, turning once, for 10 to 12 minutes or until crisp.

Chef Benjamin Davis
Cypress Club
San Francisco, CA

ABALONE FESTIVAL

MENDOCINO

Annual. October weekend varies.

Here's your chance to savor one of California's well-known gastropods and be legal about it! The California Department of Fish and Game restricts the collection and consumption of abalone through the state's sport fishing regulations. So, why not join in on a very special one-of-a-kind California festival.

Each year, a maximum of thirty-six cooks and divers prepare their best abalone recipes and compete for a variety of prizes including trips to Mexico and a wide variety of diving gear. Attendance is limited to three hundred visitors. Although there is no admission fee, a donation is requested to be used by the Department of Fish and Game for abalone research and preservation, the Bo-Cah Ama Council, and the Van Damme Docent Council.

Saturday's activities include the abalone cook-off and plenty of lively entertainment. Everyone in attendance is encouraged to vote for their abalone culinary favorite. In addition to tasting each competitor's entry and relaxing to the music of the band, you'll want to visit the information and display booths staffed by the California Department of Fish and Game. There, you'll learn a lot about licensing, coastal animals, abalone habitat, and the California state parks.

Sunday's Golden Abalone Dive is exciting for both participants and spectators. It's a chance to discover why amateur and professional divers rush to locate and retrieve the planted golden abalone shells. When they do, they're eligible to win a variety of prizes and awards. If you're a diver, take along your wet suit and join the fun. (Continued)

Due to the popularity of this festival, it's best to call early to make reservations. Whether you want to be a cook-off entrant or tasting participant, there are limited numbers of reservations, and they go quickly.

Don't get away without stopping by the souvenir booth. Pick up an Abalone Festival apron, T-shirt, or cookbook. In addition to getting a great take-home gift, you'll be contributing to several good environmental causes.

The festival takes place in Van Damme State Park, where the beach has long been a favorite of abalone divers. The park's visitor center, called "Living with the Sea," focuses on human interaction with the ocean and sea life. To get to the park, travel 3 miles south of Mendocino on California Highway 1.

GARLIC ABALONE NOODLES

To make abalone noodles: This technique eliminates the tenderizing process typically associated with making this tough mollusk edible. Access to a delicatessen meat slicer is necessary to achieve very thin slices. Partially freezing the meat will give the best results. Cut the abalone, foot first, into $1/10$-of-an-inch slices. With a very sharp knife, cut the slices into thin strips about $1/10$-of-an-inch wide.

Blanch raw strips in a large pot of rapidly boiling water by dipping about 1 cup of strips at a time in a strainer for 10 to 15 seconds while stirring. Remove and immediately place the strips into an ice-water bath and drain thoroughly. The abalone strips may be stored in the refrigerator for up to two days.

For the garlic purée, place peeled garlic cloves in a food processor or blender and fill to one cup with olive oil. Blend to a purée. Heat purée in a frying pan, $1/4$ cup of oil per cup of abalone noodles. Sauté about 1 tablespoon of garlic purée per cup noodles for 10 to 20 seconds. Add abalone noodles and stir to coat with the garlic oil. Remember the noodles are already cooked and only need to be warmed. Further cooking can toughen them. Add fresh cracked pepper and chopped parsley to taste. Garnish with Parmesan cheese and serve with sourdough French bread to soak up the garlic oil.

Randy Dexter
Mendocino, CA

Abalone noodles
1 cup peeled garlic cloves
extra virgin olive oil
cracked black pepper
parsley, chopped
Parmesan cheese, grated

THAI ABALONE HORS D'OEUVRES

Thai Abalone Meatballs

1 pound abalone, sliced, pounded tender, and ground

8 water chestnuts, chopped

2 eggs

2 inches lemon grass, chopped very fine

1 tablespoon cornstarch

1 teaspoon salt

1 teaspoon soy sauce

1 teaspoon sugar

$^1/_4$ cup flour

seasoned bread crumbs

Peanut Sauce

$^1/_2$ cup creamy peanut butter

$^1/_2$ cup coconut milk

$^1/_2$ teaspoon curry powder

2 tablespoons chopped cilantro

$^1/_4$ teaspoon powdered ginger

1 clove garlic, crushed

1 teaspoon lime juice

1 teaspoon sugar

2 tablespoons soy sauce

Coconut Curry Sauce

$^1/_2$ can cream of mushroom soup

$^3/_4$ cup coconut milk

2 inches lemon grass, chopped fine

$^1/_2$ teaspoon curry powder

$^1/_4$ teaspoon powdered ginger

1 teaspoon lime juice

1 teaspoon sugar

dash Tabasco sauce

Combine all meatball ingredients (except bread crumbs) and form into 1-inch balls. Roll in seasoned bread crumbs. Deep fry until golden brown.

To make each sauce, combine each list of ingredients separately. Simmer separately for 10 minutes. Dip meatballs in one or both sauces.

Cindy and Rod Panzer
Mendocino, CA

ABALONE TRADITIONAL

Pound whole abalone until tender. Slice into thick or thin pieces. Dip into beer and egg mixture. Roll in flour and saltine cracker crumbs or a breading of your choice. Fry in olive oil heated to near smoke for 30 to 45 seconds on each side. Season with salt, pepper, and garlic while frying. Squeeze lemon or lime juice on abalone and serve.

Dan Wilhelmi
Mendocino, CA

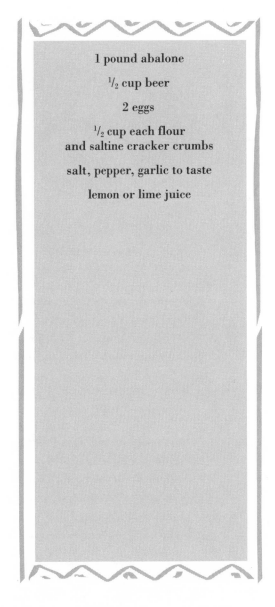

1 pound abalone

1/2 cup beer

2 eggs

1/2 cup each flour
and saltine cracker crumbs

salt, pepper, garlic to taste

lemon or lime juice

APRICOT FIESTA

PATTERSON

Annual. First weekend in June.

Now in its third decade, the Patterson Apricot Fiesta was launched to provide an occasion to celebrate the community and the apricot industry. The festival features a delectable diversity of fresh and dried apricots, jams, pies, ice cream, and yogurt.

The family-style weekend celebration presents hot air balloon launches, the Firemans' Muster, a horseshoe tournament, food booths, bingo, a petting zoo, fireworks, and plenty of free entertainment. Prominent among the many events are the Apricot Recipe Contest and the Run for Apricots Competition.

People of all ages are invited to participate in a rousing horseshoe tournament. The Fiesta Parade starts at 11 A.M., downtown, followed by the delicious Lion's Club barbecue. Activities include a breakfast in the park, and plenty of games, and sport competitions for both children and adults.

Best of all, of course, are the apricots. You'll get a chance to munch a delectable diversity of apricots along with a bountiful menu of other appealing delicacies.

Patterson, a small rural community of 9,000 people, located in the Central Valley region of California, prides itself on being the Apricot Capital of the World. Agriculture is the prime economic base of Patterson. You may want to check out several local produce stands and area farms selling locally grown fruits and vegetables. Popular home-grown items you'll discover include almonds, walnuts, pistachios, and of course, plenty of apricots.

APRICOT PIÑA COLADA

Combine all ingredients in blender. Whirl until smooth and frothy.

California Apricot Advisory Board
Walnut Creek, CA

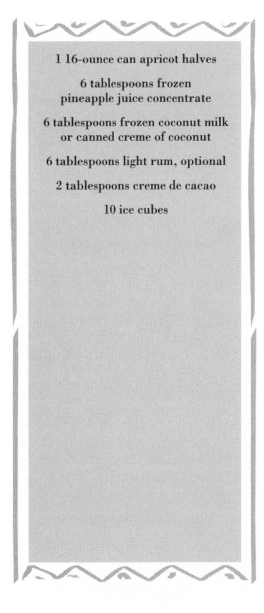

1 16-ounce can apricot halves

6 tablespoons frozen
pineapple juice concentrate

6 tablespoons frozen coconut milk
or canned creme of coconut

6 tablespoons light rum, optional

2 tablespoons creme de cacao

10 ice cubes

CHINESE APRICOT CHICKEN

1 whole chicken (4 pounds), cut up

$\frac{1}{2}$ cup rice wine vinegar or white wine vinegar

$\frac{1}{2}$ cup water

$\frac{1}{2}$ cup sugar

3 tablespoons soy sauce

2 tablespoons sherry

3 tablespoons catsup

2 tablespoons cornstarch

2 tablespoons peanut oil

6 fresh apricots, halved

3 green onions, cut into 2-inch slivers

Cut chicken parts into 2-inch pieces (use a cleaver and whack straight down through the bone). Combine vinegar, water, sugar, soy sauce, sherry, catsup, and cornstarch for sauce; set aside. In a wok, heat oil and stir-fry chicken over high heat 10 minutes or until tender and golden brown. Add apricots and stir-fry 1 minute. Pour sauce mixture over chicken and cook, stirring until thickened. Garnish with green onion slivers.

California Apricot Advisory Board
Walnut Creek, CA

STIR-FRY PORK AND APRICOTS

Cut pork into $^3/_4$-inch cubes; set aside. Mix cornstarch and soy sauce. Add pork, toss to coat. Turn into hot skillet with heated oil; stir-fry until pork is cooked, about 10 minutes. Meanwhile, drain apricots; reserve $^3/_4$ cup syrup to add to glaze sauce.

For glaze, combine cornstarch, soy sauce, white vinegar, mustard, and remaining $^3/_4$ cup apricot syrup.

Add sauce mixture to skillet; stir until lustrous. Add apricots and heat through.

California Apricot Advisory Board
Walnut Creek, CA

1 pound lean, boneless pork

1 tablespoon cornstarch

1 tablespoon soy sauce

2 tablespoons vegetable oil

1 16-ounce can apricot halves

Glaze Sauce

1 tablespoon cornstarch

1 tablespoon soy sauce

1 tablespoon white vinegar

$1^1/_2$ teaspoons Dijon mustard

DRIED APRICOT-PISTACHIO BISCOTTI

Italian Cookie

1¼ cups all-purpose flour

½ cup whole wheat flour

1 cup sugar

½ teaspoon baking powder

¼ teaspoon salt

5 tablespoons unsalted butter, cold, cut into pieces

¾ teaspoon vanilla

2 large eggs, lightly beaten

⅔ cup chopped dried apricot halves

1 cup natural California pistachios, shelled

1 teaspoon sugar

Preheat oven to 350°. Lightly butter large baking sheet. In food processor, combine flour, sugar, baking powder, and salt. Pulse to blend. Add butter and vanilla; pulse until mixture resembles coarse meal. Add eggs and pulse 3 times to blend. Add apricots and pistachios; pulse until mixture is just moistened. Transfer mixture to large bowl, use hands to form into dough. Divide dough in half.

On lightly greased baking sheet, shape dough into 2 12-inch logs. With hands, flatten each log to a width of 2 inches. Sprinkle each with remaining sugar. Bake 25 minutes or until golden brown. Remove logs to cooling rack for 10 minutes. With serrated knife, carefully cut logs on the diagonal into 1-inch slices. Place on baking sheet cut side up; return to oven and bake 7 minutes, or until lightly browned. Transfer to rack and cool completely.

California Pistachio Commission
Fresno, CA

ART A LA CARTE
MAMMOTH LAKES
Annual. September date varies.

5

The Art a la Carte festival takes place at Mammoth Creek Park and features some of Mammoth's finest restaurants. You can take your pick from a variety of foods, including smoked salmon, beef, and chicken kabobs, and andouille sausage on skewers. In addition, you'll get a chance to sample some of the area's choice wines.

Throughout the event, artwork by some of California's best artists are on display in a juried art exhibit. Some artists are on hand to discuss their work with the public. Stroll among craftspeople, artists, and jewelers displaying and selling their wares.

What would a food and wine festival be without some terrific entertainment by talented musicians? Art a la Carte is an auspicious event that blends the beauty of art and music, the magnificence of natural surroundings, and the delicacy of fine wines produced by some of California's most noted wineries.

Nestled among the pines, Mammoth Lakes' natural splendor and recreational attractions are complemented by resort accommodations offering everything from cabins to first-class hotels and condominiums. More than fifty restaurants dispense the taste of Mammoth. Shops, galleries, and boutiques deal in gifts, souvenirs, and seasonal fun in the great outdoors.

To reach the festival from U.S. Highway 395, take California Highway 203 into Mammoth. Turn left onto Old Mammoth Road and drive approximately 2.5 miles to Mammoth Creek Park.

DUCK AND WALNUT ENCHILADAS WITH TOMATILLO SAUCE AND SMOKED CHEESES

Sauce

5 pounds tomatillos - husks removed

3 tablespoons olive oil

3 cups onion, chopped

1 5-pound can green Ortega chiles, chopped

4 teaspoons chopped fresh oregano

4 cups chicken stock

3 bay leaves

1 tablespoon sugar

salt and pepper to taste

Filling

5 pounds duck leg meat, cubed or diced

salt, pepper, cumin, and chili powder to taste

5 pounds smoked cheddar cheese, grated

5 pounds smoked mozzarella cheese, grated

4 cups chopped walnuts

3 bunches chopped fresh oregano

4 dozen 6-inch flour tortillas

Cook tomatillos in boiling water for 5 minutes; drain. In separate sauté pan, heat oil and sauté onions for 5 minutes. Then purée tomatillos, cooked onions, chilies, and 1 cup of the chicken stock in food processor. Add bay leaves, sugar, salt, and pepper to taste. Return to heat for 30 minutes. Set aside.

Preheat oven to 350°. Sauté duck meat with salt, pepper, cumin, and chili powder for about 10 minutes. Slightly warm tortillas on griddle top. Brush with tomatillo sauce. Fill with duck, cheeses, walnuts, and fresh oregano. Roll and fill casserole dish. Top casserole dish of enchiladas with tomatillo sauce and cheese. Cover and heat in oven for about 20 minutes. Serve immediately.

Chef Steve Mejia
Mammoth Stonehouse Brewery and Restaurant
Mammoth Lakes, CA

 Makes 48 enchiladas.

BARBECUE CHICKEN KABOBS

Sauté onion and garlic in butter in a small saucepot over medium heat until softened. Stir in rest of barbecue sauce ingredients and simmer uncovered for 20 to 30 minutes until slightly thickened. Allow to cool. Marinate chicken in barbecue sauce for 4 to 6 hours in refrigerator. Alternate chicken cubes and vegetables on skewers. Grill over medium-hot fire for 10 to 15 minutes. May substitute beef for chicken.

Gail Hobbs, author of
Cookin' In Ventura
Ventura, CA

Barbecue Sauce

1 tablespoon butter

$1/4$ cup diced onion

1 teaspoon minced garlic

1 cup catsup

2 tablespoons each Worcestershire sauce, cider vinegar, brown sugar

1 tablespoon each hot mustard and lemon juice

$1/4$ teaspoon each salt and black pepper

4 whole chicken breasts, boneless, skinless, and cut into 1-inch cubes

1 pound fresh mushrooms

2 medium zucchini, cut into 1-inch pieces

SALMON WITH AVOCADO CREAM SAUCE

4 salmon fillets, about 6 ounces each

¼ cup soy sauce

¼ cup dry sherry

¼ cup virgin olive oil

1 tablespoon dried tarragon

salt and pepper to taste

Sauce

½ cup Alexander Valley Vineyards Chardonnay

½ tablespoon finely chopped shallot

2 cups heavy cream

½ teaspoon salt

½ teaspoon white pepper

1 large avocado

Lay salmon fillets in a flat dish. Combine soy sauce, sherry, olive oil, tarragon, salt, and pepper, and pour over salmon, turning to coat both sides. Cover and marinate in refrigerator for at least 30 minutes, turning once. Preheat oven to 425°.

To prepare sauce, place wine and shallot in a heavy saucepan and reduce by half over medium-high heat, about 5 minutes. Add cream, salt and pepper and continue cooking at a low-rolling boil, stirring occasionally, until reduced by half, about 10 minutes. Set aside to cool slightly. Peel, pit, and purée avocado and add to cooled sauce. For a smoother sauce, pass through a sieve. Place salmon fillets on a rack in a small baking pan and season with salt and pepper. Bake for 8 to 10 minutes, depending on thickness of fish. Serve with sauce.

Alexander Valley Vineyards 1993 Chardonnay
Cuisine Cuisien Catering
San Francisco, CA

GRILLED POLENTA WITH SONOMA JACK CHEESE

In large saucepan, bring stock seasoned with salt to taste, white pepper, and thyme to a boil. Slowly beat in polenta or cornmeal with a whisk to avoid lumps. Reduce heat to low and stir to prevent sticking. Cook slowly for 10 minutes.

In separate skillet, heat 2 tablespoons of the butter. Sauté minced mushrooms and scallions until just starting to brown, about 5 minutes. Season with a little salt and pepper, add wine, and reduce until most of the wine cooks away. Add to polenta mixture with remaining 6 tablespoons of butter and the parsley.

Butter large shallow dish or baking sheet. Spread polenta mixture in the dish to a depth of $1/2$ inch and smooth top. Cool, cover with plastic wrap, and refrigerate. Can be made one or two days ahead of time.

Cut polenta into 4-inch diamonds. Grill until surface is lightly toasted. Turn, cover with a slice of jack cheese, and grill until cheese is just starting to melt. Serve warm, garnished with grilled shiitake mushrooms and slivers of sun-dried tomatoes.

John Ash and Company Restaurant
Santa Rosa, CA

1 quart chicken stock or canned chicken broth

salt (to taste)

2 teaspoons ground white pepper

1 teaspoon minced fresh thyme

1 cup polenta or yellow cornmeal

8 tablespoons butter

$1/2$ cup minced mushrooms

$1/2$ cup minced scallions

salt and freshly ground black pepper

$1/2$ cup Alexander Valley Vineyards Chardonnay

1 tablespoon minced fresh parsley

$1/3$ pound sliced Sonoma jack cheese

$1/3$ pound fresh shiitake mushrooms, grilled or sautéed in butter, for garnish

1 ounce sun-dried tomatoes packed in oil, drained, and slivered, for garnish

ART & PUMPKIN FESTIVAL
HALF MOON BAY
Annual. October weekend following Columbus Day.

6

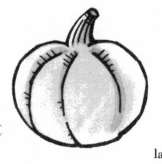

If fine art and fine food appeal to you, then you'll find your artistic and culinary fantasies satisfied at this first-rate tribute in festival form. The Great Pumpkin takes center stage at the annual Half Moon Bay Art & Pumpkin Festival. The admission-free event features three hundred artists and craftspeople, along with tables laden with savory foods and scrumptious pumpkin specialties. Two stages provide entertainment.

The festival centers around street performers, a children's stage, a haunted house, and giant carved pumpkins. Special events include the Costume Contest, Great Pumpkin Parade, Pumpkin Pie Eating Contest, Pumpkin Carving Contest, glittering Masquerade Ball, 10K fun run, and the Great Pumpkin Weigh-Off.

Half Moon Bay is located in San Mateo County, 25 miles south of San Francisco along California Highway 1. Getting to Half Moon Bay is part of the fun. You'll travel scenic highways 1, 84, and 92 through oceanside farm country dotted with scarecrows and pick-your-own pumpkin patches.

This famous old farming and fishing community sports a bustling harbor, bountiful fields of Brussels sprouts and pumpkins, lush countryside, and friendly people. Around town, you'll discover dozens of pumpkin patches and quaint shops where you can purchase pumpkins and pumpkin-related goodies.

PUMPKIN CAKE ROLL

Preheat oven to 375°. Grease and flour 15x10x1-inch jelly roll pan. Beat eggs on high speed for 5 minutes, gradually beat in granulated sugar. Stir in pumpkin and lemon juice. Sift together flour, baking powder, cinnamon, ginger, nutmeg, and salt. Fold into pumpkin mixture. Spread into prepared pan. Top with walnuts. Bake for 15 minutes. Sprinkle powdered sugar onto a dish cloth and turn cake out onto cloth. Starting at narrow end, roll towel and cake together, cool, and unroll.

For filling, combine powdered sugar, cream cheese, butter, and vanilla. Beat until smooth. Spread over cake, roll up, and chill.

Art & Pumpkin Festival
Half Moon Bay, CA

 This dessert freezes well.

3 eggs

1 cup sugar

$^2/_3$ cup pumpkin

1 teaspoon lemon juice

$^3/_4$ cup flour

1 teaspoon baking powder

2 teaspoons cinnamon

1 teaspoon ginger

$^1/_2$ teaspoon nutmeg

$^1/_2$ teaspoon salt

1 cup finely chopped walnuts

powdered sugar

Filling

1 cup powdered sugar

1 6-ounce package of cream cheese

4 teaspoons butter

$^1/_2$ teaspoon vanilla

CHOCOLATE CHIP PUMPKIN LOAF

1 cup plus 2 tablespoons flour

$1/2$ teaspoon baking powder

$1/2$ teaspoon baking soda

$1/4$ teaspoon salt

$1/2$ teaspoon each ground cinnamon, nutmeg, ginger, and allspice

1 egg

$1/2$ cup oil

1 teaspoon vanilla extract

$3/4$ cup sugar

1 cup canned pumpkin

$3/4$ cup chopped walnuts

$3/4$ cup chocolate chips

confectioners sugar, optional

Sift together flour, baking powder, baking soda, salt, and spices. Set aside. Beat egg, oil, vanilla, and sugar together in a medium mixing bowl. Stir in pumpkin. Add in $1/4$ of the flour mixture at a time and mix very well by hand. Stir in nuts and chocolate chips. Bake in a greased and floured loaf pan for about 45 minutes in a 350° oven until tester comes out clean. Allow to cool before removing from pan. Dust with confectioners sugar, if desired.

Gail Hobbs
Ventura, CA

PICKLED PUMPKIN

Prepare a syrup using vinegar and sugar. Combine dry spices in cheesecloth bag. Add spices to syrup and bring to boil for 5 minutes. Cook pumpkin in syrup until tender. Put pumpkin in storage containers, cover with syrup, and seal.

Barbara Weber
Oak View, CA

 Pumpkins grow in several agricultural regions scattered throughout California. The pickling process allows for year-round use.

1 quart white vinegar

4 pounds sugar

1 teaspoon whole cloves

1 tablespoon coarsely broken cinnamon stick

5 pounds pumpkin, peeled, cut into 1-inch pieces

ASPARAGUS FESTIVAL

STOCKTON

Annual. Fourth weekend in April.

7

The annual celebration of the spring asparagus harvest takes place in the picturesque Oak Grove Regional Park in Stockton. There's always plenty of entertainment and delicious food to satisfy anyone's taste buds. Asparagus Alley is where any gourmand wants to be. It's filled with mouth-watering asparagus pasta, deep-fried asparagus, asparagus sandwiches, steamed asparagus, and more.

One of several activities taking place during the festival is the Concours d'Elegance, where car buffs goggle at more than two hundred cars of all makes and vintages. The spit-and-polish vehicles are displayed for everyone to enjoy and admire. Rounding out the festival, dozens of art and craft vendors offer jewelry, pottery, textiles, leather products, paintings, and photography.

Entertainment is provided at the Asparagus Festival Main Entertainment Stage, the Country Entertainment Pavilion, and Children's Entertainment Amphitheater. In addition, strolling musicians, barbershop quartets, and magicians perform throughout the festival grounds.

The original Stockton asparagus cookbook, *Asparagus All Ways...Always,* is filled with festival recipes, including the ones that follow.

ASPARA-KOPITAS

Sauté, in frying pan with oil, the asparagus, onion, bell pepper or pimento, garlic, and mushrooms until half cooked. Season with herbs and deglaze with wine or vermouth. Allow the mixture to cool for 10 minutes.

Unfold the pastry dough, then cut each sheet into 9 equal squares, yielding a total of 18 pieces. The defrosted dough can be easily rolled and should be rolled out a little thinner. Place a spoonful of the mixture onto a sheet of dough; sprinkle with cheese. Place another sheet on top and crimp the edges with a fork. Brushing the edges with egg white or water helps to seal them. Trim excess dough to square it. Brush each aspara-kopita with egg white before baking. Bake at 375° for about 15 minutes, or until puffed and lightly brown.

These may be served either warm or at room temperature. This appetizer is fashioned after spanikopeta, the Greek spinach and feta cheese pie.

Steve Clement
Grand Prize Winner at Asparagus Festival
Stockton, CA

 This appetizer is easy to make, has bold flavors, is elegant for parties, and may be prepared ahead of time.

olive oil

1½ pounds fresh asparagus, cleaned, trimmed, and cut into ½-inch diagonal pieces

¼ onion, minced

½ marinated red bell pepper, or pimento

3 cloves garlic, minced, or garlic powder

½ cup sliced mushrooms

tarragon or Provençal herbs, to taste

dash white wine or vermouth

1 package frozen puff pastry dough (Pepperidge Farm) (2 sheets)

8 ounces feta cheese, or favorite cheese

egg white, optional

SAN JOAQUIN VALLEY ENCHILADAS

2 to 3 pounds fresh asparagus

$^1/_2$ cup oil

12 tortillas

$^1/_2$ cup butter

$^1/_2$ cup flour

$^3/_4$ cup chicken broth

1 cup sour cream

$^1/_2$ cup green taco sauce

3 cups grated jack cheese

3 cups cooked, shredded chicken

$^1/_2$ cup onion, chopped

Parmesan cheese

Blanch and drain asparagus, cut into 1-inch pieces, set aside. Cook each tortilla in a large oiled skillet to soften. Set aside to cool and drain. In saucepan, melt butter, blend in flour, and add chicken broth. Cook until thick and bubbly, stirring constantly. Add sour cream and taco sauce. Heat thoroughly.

Fill each tortilla with a handful of jack cheese, chicken, onion, asparagus, and 3 tablespoons sauce. Roll tortilla. Place seam-side down in glass dish. When all tortillas have been filled, sprinkle with any remaining cheese. Top with a layer of Parmesan cheese and the remaining sauce. Bake at 425° for 25 minutes.

Liz Rotert
Grand Prize Winner at Asparagus Festival
Stockton, CA

ASPARAGUS POPPY SEED LOAF

Combine all streusel ingredients, mix until crumbly. Set aside.

Sift together flour, salt, baking powder, and baking soda. Set aside. In a large mixing bowl, beat the butter, eggs, and sugar until well blended (about 3 minutes). Mix in sour cream, vanilla, cream sherry, and poppy seeds until well mixed. Fold in sifted ingredients and asparagus. Pour batter into a 9x5-inch loaf pan that has been lightly buttered and floured. Evenly sprinkle streusel on mixture.

Bake at 375° for 55 to 60 minutes, or until toothpick inserted into center comes out clean.

David Bardo
Second Prize Winner at Asparagus Festival
Stockton, CA

Streusel Topping
$^1/_4$ cup sugar

$^1/_4$ cup brown sugar, lightly packed

1 tablespoon flour

2 tablespoons butter,
room temperature

Loaf
2 cups flour

$^1/_2$ teaspoon salt

$^3/_4$ teaspoon baking powder

$^1/_2$ teaspoon baking soda

$^1/_4$ cup butter, room temperature

2 eggs, room temperature

$^3/_4$ cup sugar

1 cup sour cream

$1^1/_2$ teaspoons vanilla extract

$^1/_4$ cup cream sherry

$^1/_4$ cup poppy seeds

6 ounces fresh asparagus tips,
cleaned and finely chopped

ASPARAGUS LASAGNA

1 to 2 pounds fresh asparagus,
cut into pieces

3 tablespoons butter

2 green onions, chopped

12 ounces fresh mushrooms, chopped

$1/4$ cup flour

1 teaspoon salt

$1/4$ teaspoon cayenne pepper

$2^1/2$ cups milk

8 ounces lasagna noodles

black pepper

2 cups cottage cheese

8 ounces jack cheese, shredded

$1/2$ to 1 cup grated Parmesan cheese

Cook asparagus, drain, and let cool. Melt butter in medium saucepan. Add onions and mushrooms, cook over medium heat, stirring occasionally, until tender, about 5 minutes. Blend in flour, salt, and cayenne pepper. Gradually stir in milk. Cook sauce until thickened for an additional 5 minutes.

Cook lasagna noodles, following package directions. Spread $1/2$ cup mushroom sauce in greased 13x9-inch baking pan. Layer noodles, seasoned with black pepper, with asparagus, cottage cheese, jack cheese, $1/3$ remaining mushroom sauce, and Parmesan cheese. Repeat to make three layers. Bake in preheated oven at 325° for 45 minutes. Let stand 20 minutes before cutting to serve.

Liz Rotert
Grand Prize Winner at Asparagus Festival
Stockton, CA

AUTUMN FOOD & WINE JUBILEE

SQUAW VALLEY

Annual. November weekend.

8

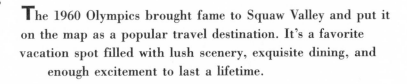

The 1960 Olympics brought fame to Squaw Valley and put it on the map as a popular travel destination. It's a favorite vacation spot filled with lush scenery, exquisite dining, and enough excitement to last a lifetime.

Here's your perfect chance to taste some of the finest Northern California wines and regional cuisine while enjoying the beautiful backdrop of the majestic Sierras and the cerulean blue of nearby Lake Tahoe.

You're invited to meander through more than thirty booths filled with gourmet foods. They're paired with fine wine, champagne, or dessert wine for your palate's pleasure.

During the jubilee, each food and wine pairing is judged by noted food and wine professionals. Awards are presented in both individual and companion categories. In recent years, the following wineries have participated: Carmanet, Caymus, Calone, Edna Valley, Fetzer, Jorand, Robert Mondavi, Mumm Cuvee, Silver Oak, Sterling, ZD, and more.

If you wish, there's a silent auction held for the serious connoisseur who wants to bid on quality items such as original artwork, fine wines, and fabulous vacation getaways. A percentage of the proceeds benefits local school art programs. The event includes a free art show.

Each year, the Autumn Food & Wine Jubilee has become more popular and often sells out, so it's wise to make early reservations in order to avoid disappointment.

ROASTED MIWOK SALMON

2 8-ounce king salmon fillets, purchase fresh with no skin and no bones

Marinade
1/2 cup white wine

1 tablespoon honey

3 or 4 dried juniper berries

10 to 12 fresh blackberries

Nut Crust
1 ounce walnuts

1 ounce pine nuts

2 ounces bread crumbs

pinch of salt and pepper

Pepper Medley
1 tablespoon safflower oil

1/2 small red onion

1/2 small red bell pepper

1/2 small yellow bell pepper

1/2 small green bell pepper

1/2 teaspoon chopped garlic

1/2 teaspoon chopped fresh sage

1 tablespoon maple syrup

Combine all ingredients for the marinade, then marinate fish for 2 to 3 hours. Toast walnuts and pine nuts in the oven until lightly browned. Pulse in a food processor with bread crumbs and salt and pepper for 3 to 4 seconds to achieve a rough texture. Remove fish from marinade and coat liberally on both sides with the nut mixture. Roast in 375° oven for 10 to 12 minutes or until cooked to preference.

Julienne the red onion and peppers. Sauté in oil with garlic and sage until lightly browned. Add the maple syrup and allow the sugar mixture to caramelize slightly. Top the roasted salmon with the pepper medley and serve.

Chef Steve Frisch
River Ranch
Tahoe City, CA

 This recipe was inspired by a combination of Native American recipes. It pairs with Grgich Hills Chardonnay.

WILD MUSHROOM PIZZA WITH POLENTA FENNEL CRUST

To prepare dough, place warm tap water in nonreactive container. Dissolve yeast and barley syrup in water and leave for 10 minutes until frothy. Add all remaining dough ingredients. This can be stirred with a wooden spoon or placed in bowl of a mixer with a dough hook attachment. Place ball of dough in covered container and let rest until it has doubled in volume. Scale dough out into 5-ounce portions. Let rest for 15 minutes, covered.

Roll dough out into flat pizza shapes about eight inches in diameter, brush with additional olive oil, place on baking stone or cookie sheet, and bake in preheated 375° oven for 12 minutes. Let cool and set aside. Pizza shells can be topped or placed in plastic zippered baggie and frozen for later use.

To prepare filling, clean mushrooms and set aside. (Shiitakes may be substituted if you're unable to find chanterelles.) Chop pancetta and sauté for 5 minutes in the olive oil and butter. Add garlic and shallots and sauté 5 minutes more. Remove pancetta and set aside. Add mushrooms and sauté on low for 10 minutes. Add tamari soy sauce, lemon juice, seasoning salt, and wine to taste. Cook 5 minutes more. Top pizza with as much or as little cheese as you care for. Arrange mushrooms on top and sprinkle with thyme and pancetta. Put in oven and bake 10 minutes or until cheese melts and crust is crisp.

Chef Bary Bulmer
Earthly Delights
Truckee, CA

 Serve this pizza with Stag's Leap Petite Syrah wine.

Dough

1 cup warm tap water, 85°

1 teaspoon Red Star yeast

1 teaspoon malted barley syrup

$^1/_2$ cup polenta

3 cups organic unbleached white flour

$^1/_4$ cup olive oil

1 tablespoon whole fennel seed

1 teaspoon ground fennel seed

pinch sea salt

Topping

2 tablespoons olive oil

1 tablespoon sweet butter

$^1/_4$ pound pancetta

1 tablespoon minced garlic

1 tablespoon minced shallots

1 pound chanterelle mushrooms

1 tablespoon tamari soy sauce

1 tablespoon fresh-squeezed lemon juice

1 teaspoon seasoning salt

Stag's Leap 1991 Petite Syrah to taste

$^1/_4$ pound grated Fontina cheese

1 tablespoon fresh lemon thyme

ROAST PORK WITH BRANDIED APPLES

1¹/₂ pounds pork tenderloin

¹/₂ cup Merlot wine

¹/₂ cup melted butter

4 tablespoons sweet butter

6 Granny Smith apples, peeled, cut into thin slices

8 ounces hazelnuts, chopped

2 sprigs fresh rosemary, chopped

4 tablespoons honey

4 to 6 ounces Kirsch brandy

Roast pork with Merlot wine and melted butter in 400° oven for 20 minutes or until tender. Sauté apples in butter for 5 minutes. Add hazelnuts, rosemary, and honey. Cook another 10 to 15 minutes, until apples are soft but not mushy. Finish with the Kirsch brandy.

When pork is finished roasting, slice into medallions. Pour apples over medallions to serve.

Chef Jami Janes
Alpenhaus
Tahoma, CA

 This dish was paired with Raymond Vineyards & Cellars Cabernet Sauvignon at Jubilee.

BLACKBERRY FESTIVAL

LAKE COUNTY

Annual. Second Saturday in August.

9

Here's an opportunity for the entire family to spend a day steeped in living history and more blackberries than you can imagine. Festival participants in early-1900s costume offer demonstrations and tours at the festival site, Anderson Marsh State Historic Park.

Visitors can tour the historic ranch house, enjoy European, Native American, and Mexican culture, and have plenty of opportunities to eat! You can start with biscuits and gravy for breakfast, and spend the remainder of the day eating everything loaded with blackberries. But a word of warning: leave room for the festival's favorite tradition, blackberry pie topped with loads of ice cream.

Throughout the day, and scattered around the festival site, you'll experience a variety of musical entertainment, dancing, and ethnic foods. There are tours of several miles of nature trails, so you'll get a chance to view wildlife, plants, and a reconstructed Native American village. Quoting a park handout, "The park contains 27 Native American archaeological sites, some as much as 10,000 years old."

Blackberries top the list on the festival's varied menu. Don't be surprised to discover a variety of blackberry pies and cobblers, ice cream, plus jams and jellies. No matter your age, you'll be as excited as a kid in a candy store.

Lake County is located approximately 100 miles north of San Francisco and 20 miles east of U.S. Highway 101. The 870-acre Anderson Marsh State Historic Park is below Lower Lake and Clear Lake on California State Highway 53.

BLACKBERRY AND APPLE CRUMBLE A LA MODE

³/₄ cup flour

¹/₄ cup brown sugar

¹/₄ cup butter, softened

1 cup walnuts, chopped

2¹/₂ pounds (approximately 6)
Granny Smith apples,
peeled and cored

juice of ¹/₂ lemon

2 cups blackberries, fresh or frozen

2 tablespoons flour

¹/₂ cup granulated sugar

1 tablespoon grated lemon zest

premium quality vanilla ice cream

Mix flour, brown sugar, and butter together with a fork until crumbly to make topping. Stir in walnuts and set aside. Slice apples thin and toss with lemon juice. Add blackberries, sprinkle with flour, sugar, and lemon zest. Mix gently. Place mixture in a 9-inch pie plate, cover with crumbled topping. Bake, uncovered, in a 350° oven for approximately 45 minutes or until golden brown on top and bubbling hot.

Gail Hobbs
Ventura, CA

 Cool slightly and serve with a scoop of your favorite vanilla ice cream.

BLACKBERRIES 'N' CREAM

Wash and pick over blackberries. In a saucepan, combine blackberries, water, sugar, and cinnamon. Bring to a boil. Reduce heat and gently simmer 10 minutes. Mix cornstarch paste into hot blackberry mixture and cook, stirring until slightly thickened (about 5 minutes). Allow to cool. Top with whipped cream and serve.

Gail Hobbs
Ventura, CA

4 cups fresh blackberries

$^1/_2$ cup hot water

1 cup sugar

$^1/_2$ teaspoon cinnamon

2 tablespoons cornstarch mixed
with 3 tablespoons water

dash of salt

1 cup heavy cream, whipped

BLACKBERRY PRESERVES

2 pounds fresh blackberries

1 pound fresh apples, peeled, cored, and chopped

4 cups sugar

Combine room-temperature berries, apples, and sugar. Bring to boil slowly, stirring until sugar dissolves. Cook rapidly until jelled. Remove from heat and skim foam from top. Allow to cool. Ladle into freezer containers and freeze.

Mavis Caffrey
Pine Mountain, CA

 These easy-to-prepare blackberry preserves allow you to enjoy the flavor of fresh berries all year long.

CHERRY BLOSSOM FESTIVAL

LODI

Annual. April weekend.

For several years the folks around Lodi have pulled out all the stops and made a special effort to entertain visitors during the Cherry Blossom Festival. Spectacular pink and white cherry blossoms greet visitors as they enter Micke Grove Regional Park, site of this annual celebration of the blossoms and the fruit they bring. The two-day activities begin around noon and last until 5 P.M. each day. For your enjoyment, Micke Grove Regional Park has picnic facilities, amusement rides, a museum, a zoo, and a Japanese garden.

Highlights of the festival are many. Most events spotlight traditional Japanese culture and feature bonsai demonstrations, entertainment, and exhibits. Food offerings include traditional cherry favorites, along with culinary treats with an oriental flavor.

In keeping with the cherry blossom theme, you'll not only eat oriental food delicacies, but soak up the sounds of Japanese music, be entertained by martial arts, and observe traditional regalia worn by festival performers and visitors as well.

Don't worry about the kids getting bored. Youngsters of all ages will get a kick out of learning about Japanese origami. You'll get a chance to make your own animals and other objects by folding sheets of paper into shapes. Still practiced in Japan, the art of origami began there in the 10th century.

To reach Micke Grove Regional Park, take the Harney Lane exit off of California Highway 99. Travel east about 2 miles and follow signs to the park.

BEEFY BAKED BEANS

1 pound lean ground beef

2 16-ounce cans pork and beans
in tomato sauce

1 15-ounce can kidney beans,
drained

1 cup catsup

1 1³/₈-ounce envelope dry onion
soup mix

¹/₂ cup water

2 tablespoons prepared mustard

2 teaspoons cider vinegar

2 cups frozen unsweetened
tart cherries

In a skillet over medium heat, cook ground beef until browned. Drain fat and add pork and beans, kidney beans, catsup, dry soup mix, water, mustard, and vinegar to meat. Mix well, stirring in cherries (frozen or thawed). Pour meat mixture into a 2¹/₂-quart baking dish. Bake in a preheated 400° oven for 30 minutes, stirring occasionally. Note: 1 cup dried tart cherries can be substituted for frozen tart cherries.

Cherry Marketing Institute
Okemos, MI

 This one-dish casserole is perfect for potlucks, family gatherings, and camping.

NO-BAKE CHERRY CHEESE SQUARES

In a medium bowl, combine graham cracker crumbs, $^1/_4$ cup sugar, and melted butter; mix well. Press crumb mixture firmly into the bottom of a 9x9x2-inch baking pan. Let crust chill while preparing the rest of the ingredients. In a mixing bowl with an electric mixer, combine cream cheese, remaining $^1/_4$ cup sugar, lemon peel, and vanilla; beat until light and fluffy. Fold in whipped topping. Pour into prepared crust. Combine cherry filling and almond extract. Pour over cheese filling. Let chill.

Cherry Marketing Institute
Okemos, MI

$1^1/_4$ cups graham cracker crumbs

$^1/_2$ cup granulated sugar

$^1/_3$ cup butter or margarine, melted

1 3-ounce package cream cheese, softened

2 teaspoons grated lemon peel

1 teaspoon vanilla extract

2 cups frozen whipped topping, thawed

1 21-ounce can cherry filling and topping

$^1/_2$ teaspoon almond extract

SWEET CHERRY SAUCE IN MERINGUE SHELLS

3 cups fresh sweet Northwest cherries, pitted and halved

2 tablespoons orange juice

$^1/_2$ teaspoon almond extract

$^1/_4$ teaspoon cream of tartar

dash salt

3 egg whites (room temperature)

1 cup sugar

Toss cherries with orange juice and refrigerate to completely chill. Add almond extract, cream of tartar, and salt to egg whites, beating until frothy. Gradually add sugar, beating until very stiff peaks form and sugar is completely dissolved. Cover baking sheet with ungreased plain or parchment paper; draw eight $3^1/_2$-inch circles on paper. Spread each circle with $^1/_3$ cup meringue; shape with back of spoon to make shells. Bake for 1 hour at 275°. Turn off heat, leave meringues in oven $1^1/_2$ hours longer. Fill each meringue shell with cherries.

Northwest Cherry Growers
Yakima, WA

CHERRY AND WINE SAUCE

Remove stems from cherries. Combine cherries, orange juice, wine, sugar, and peel. Cover and bring to a boil. Allow to cool slightly. Snip cherries with scissors and remove pits with a fork. Combine water and cornstarch, stir into cherry mixture. Cook and stir until thickened.

Northwest Cherry Growers
Yakima, WA

2 cups frozen sweet Northwest cherries

3 tablespoons orange juice

3 tablespoons red wine

$1/_4$ cup sugar

1 tablespoon grated orange peel

1 tablespoon cold water

2 teaspoons cornstarch

CHILI COOK-OFF

WILLOW CREEK

Annual. Held on Father's Day in June.

11

If you love good chili, you'll want to attend Willow Creek's annual Chili Cook-off. Each of the tasty entries is judged by a panel of experts, with rewards and recognitions given. But the most fun comes, and real competition gets keen, as amateur cooks vie for the most popular chili during the event's annual "ballot box stuffing" contest. If you find a chili you especially like, you can buy ballots and stuff the bucket provided by that entrant. The money goes to help support the local China Flat Museum, and the more ballots you buy the more votes your personal favorite gets. Got the idea?

Willow Creek is located near where California Highways 299 and 96 meet in Northern California. It's a place where you can fish for salmon, enjoy scenic rivers, swim at the beach, hike in the backcountry, and drive along the Trinity Scenic Byway. The Cook-off is held on the Musuem grounds. Anyone in Willow Creek (population less than 1,500) will happily point you in the right direction if you miss it.

During the last quarter century, the lore of the legendary creature known as Bigfoot has been the topic of many stories around Willow Creek. In 1935, huge tracks were found in the snow on a nearby mountain. You'll find a large statue of Bigfoot in the heart of town. After a day of chili feasting, you may feel the urge to join in the controversy of determining if Bigfoot is really a wildman or simply a legend.

BROWNIE'S SWEET VENISON CHILI

Mix ingredients and bring to a boil. Simmer 2 hours. Grate sharp cheese over top before serving.

Orville Brown
Willow Creek, CA

4 cups cooked pinto beans

1-pound can stewed tomatoes

1 cup brown sugar

2 tablespoons cumin

3 pounds venison, cut into small pieces

2 large yellow onions, diced

1 can salsa, medium

1 can salsa, hot

1 green onion, chopped

$\frac{1}{2}$ cup Worcestershire sauce

2 tablespoons lemon pepper

$\frac{1}{2}$ cup chopped fresh parsley

2 tablespoons seasoned salt

4 cups water

1 quart chicken stock

sharp cheese, optional

CHILI BEANS

$1^1/_2$ pounds hamburger or ground venison

1 green bell pepper, chopped

1 medium onion, chopped

1 quart tomatoes

1 8-ounce can tomato sauce

2 small bay leaves

4 teaspoons chili powder

salt, pepper, paprika, to taste

1 pound cooked kidney beans

Brown meat in heavy skillet. Add green bell pepper and onion. Cook until tender. Add tomatoes, tomato sauce, and seasonings. Cook slowly for 2 hours. Add water to keep right consistency. Remove bay leaves and add beans the last $1/_2$ hour of cooking.

Shirley Keyes
Willow Creek, CA

 Lightly season beans before cooking.

SPICY CALIFORNIA CHILI

Cook onion and beef over medium-high heat. Add remaining ingredients. Simmer on low heat approximately 20 minutes. Stir occasionally. Remove bay leaf before serving. Variation: ground turkey may be substituted for beef. Try doubling ingredients and freezing.

Bob Carter
Oxnard, CA

Serve with a crisp salad and a French roll.

1 pound ground beef

$\frac{1}{2}$ cup onion, chopped

1 16-ounce can Italian-style tomatoes with oregano and basil

1 6-ounce can tomato sauce

2 teaspoons chili powder

1 teaspoon Worcestershire sauce

1 teaspoon white wine vinegar

1 large bay leaf

salt and pepper to taste

$\frac{1}{2}$ teaspoon garlic powder

1 teaspoon cumin

dash of crushed red pepper or $\frac{1}{2}$ teaspoon Tabasco sauce

CHOCOLATE FESTIVAL
OAKDALE
Annual. Weekend following Mother's Day in May.

12

Hershey Chocolate U.S.A. has celebrated more than thirty years in Oakdale. What better way to recognize the importance of the company than to hold an annual Oakdale Chocolate Festival? Forget the bathroom scale just this once. The family-oriented Oakdale Chocolate Festival is two days filled with fabulous food, fun, entertainment, and chocolate, chocolate, chocolate.

This festival is complete with Kid's Land, tours of the local Hershey Plant on Saturday, entertainment on two stages, classic car shows, a tennis tournament, the three-mile Truffle Trot, arts and crafts, food of every variety, and vendors selling or giving away all manner of chocolate products. Chocolate Avenue sells (and gives tastings of) everything from Hershey's Peanut Butter Cups to fudge, brownies, ice cream, truffles, chocolate cotton candy, and even chocolate gummy bears.

The Hershey Visitor Center is located in downtown Oakdale. Catch the shuttle from the visitor center to the Hershey Plant for a tour. (Tours offered throughout the year.) Following the tour, you'll be returned to the visitor center where you can browse through exhibits and feast your eyes upon freshly baked chocolate chip cookies and a full line of chocolate and confectionery products.

CHOCO-LIGHT MUFFINS

Heat oven to 400°. Line 2½-inch diameter muffin tin with paper cups. In medium bowl, stir together flour, sugar, cocoa, baking powder, baking soda, and salt. Stir in yogurt, milk, and vanilla just until combined. Do not beat. Fill each cup ⅔ full with batter. Bake 15 to 20 minutes or just until wooden pick inserted in center comes out clean. Cool slightly in pan on wire rack. Sprinkle with powdered sugar, if desired. Serve warm.

Hershey Kitchens
Hershey, PA

1½ cups flour

¾ cup sugar

¼ cup Hershey's cocoa or European-style cocoa

2 teaspoons baking powder

1 teaspoon baking soda

½ teaspoon salt

⅔ cup vanilla lowfat yogurt

⅔ cup skim milk

½ teaspoon vanilla extract

powdered sugar, optional

HERSHEY'S COCOA CREAM PIE

Snow Ghost Cream Pie

1/2 cup Hershey's cocoa

1 1/4 cups sugar

1/3 cup cornstarch

1/4 teaspoon salt

3 cups milk

3 tablespoons butter or margarine

1 1/2 teaspoons vanilla extract

1 baked 9-inch pie crust or graham cracker crumb crust, cooled

sweetened whipped cream

In medium saucepan, stir together cocoa, sugar, cornstarch, and salt. Gradually blend milk into dry ingredients, stirring until smooth. Cook over medium heat, stirring constantly, until mixture boils; boil 1 minute. Remove from heat and stir in butter and vanilla. Pour into baked pie crust. Carefully press plastic wrap directly onto pie filling. Cool, then refrigerate 6 to 8 hours. Top with whipped cream.

Hershey Kitchens
Hershey, PA

WHITE CHOCOLATE-FIG PIE

Finely chop figs by hand or in food processor. Process until smooth, or beat well, with melted chocolate, half-and-half, and eggs. Pour into prepared crust. Bake in preheated 350° oven until knife inserted off-center comes out clean, about 30 to 35 minutes. Let cool completely. Refrigerate.

California Fig Advisory Board
Fresno, CA

$1\frac{1}{2}$ cups California figs,
stems removed

1 12-ounce package white chocolate,
melted

$\frac{2}{3}$ cup half-and-half

2 eggs

1 8-inch graham cracker or
chocolate crumb crust

DEEP DARK CHOCOLATE CAKE

2 cups sugar

1³/₄ cups all-purpose flour

³/₄ cup Hershey's cocoa or Hershey's European-style cocoa

1¹/₂ teaspoons baking powder

1¹/₂ teaspoons baking soda

1 teaspoon salt

2 eggs

1 cup milk

¹/₂ cup vegetable oil

2 teaspoons vanilla extract

1 cup boiling water

Buttercream Frosting

6 tablespoons butter or margarine, softened

2²/₃ cups powdered sugar

¹/₂ cup Hershey's cocoa or Hershey's European-style cocoa

¹/₃ cup milk

1 teaspoon vanilla extract

Heat oven to 350°. Grease and flour two 9-inch round pans or a 13x9x2-inch baking pan. In large mixer bowl, stir together sugar, flour, cocoa, baking powder, baking soda, and salt. Add eggs, milk, oil, and vanilla. Beat on medium speed of electric mixer 2 minutes. Remove from mixer and stir in boiling water (batter will be thin). Pour batter into pans. Bake 30 to 35 minutes for round pans, 35 to 40 minutes for rectangular pan, or until wooden pick inserted in center comes out clean. Cool ten minutes and remove from pans to wire rack. Cake may be left in rectangular pan, if desired. Cool completely and add frosting.

To prepare frosting, in small mixer bowl, beat butter and add powdered sugar and cocoa alternately with milk. Beat to spreading consistency, adding additional milk if necessary. Blend in vanilla.

Hershey Kitchens
Hershey, PA

 This recipe has appeared on the Hershey's cocoa can for many years.

CLAM CHOWDER COOK-OFF

SANTA CRUZ

Annual. February weekend varies.

13

If you're a clam chowder aficionado you don't want to miss this cook-off, one of California's best food competitions. It is held, without a doubt, at one of the state's most enduring and fun festival sites. Whether red and brothy or white and creamy, chowder takes top billing at the annual cook-off held at the Santa Cruz Beach Boardwalk.

Up to sixty teams from throughout California enter this popular seaside cook-off. Team members concoct a variety of strategies to win the top award in both red and white chowder categories.

Admission to the boardwalk and the cook-off is free. If you want to sample chowders, you need to purchase a tasting kit. You'll want to hang around about 10 A.M. to observe as the chefs begin their often flamboyant preparation of ingredients. At 1 P.M. the public sampling and the voting for the popular People's Choice award begins.

Prizes are awarded not only for best chowder, but for team spirit as well. That spirit is shown off by costumed chefs dressed as clams, mermaids, King Neptune, various sea creatures, and the infamous Clam Fairy. You'll be treated to hilarious shenanigans along with many taste treats.

On Sunday, no doubt to work off some of the delicious clam chowder, runners enter the annual Great Chowder Chase, a 4.5-mile race in the beach area. The chase often draws more than one thousand runners.

The seaside resort community of Santa Cruz boasts nearly thirty miles of public beach.

BEST RESTAURANT MANHATTAN CHOWDER

3 pounds raw diced smoked bacon, chopped

8 green bell peppers, diced

8 red bell peppers, diced

6 large yellow onions, diced

12 carrots, diced

2 large bunches celery, diced

2 cups diced garlic

2 cups diced shallots

6 bunches of leeks, diced

1 gallon port wine

$^1/_2$ 10-pound can tomato paste

3 10-pound cans diced tomatoes in juice

6 bay leaves

3 tablespoons gumbo powder

4 tablespoons Italian seasoning

3 tablespoons garlic powder

salt and pepper to taste

2 bunches fresh chopped basil

8 1-quart cans clam juice

7 1-quart cans chopped clams in juice

24 russet potatoes, diced, steamed until soft

3 cups lemon juice

1 cup sugar

3 cups dark roux

Sauté bacon, then all vegetables; deglaze with wine and reduce. Add all tomato products, all spices, then add all other ingredients. Cook for 1 $^1/_2$ hours. Adjust for final tasting with additional sugar, salt, pepper, and lemon juice.

Chef Steve Cazel
Severino's Restaurant
1st Place Winner

Unless you are serving a crowd, you may want to reduce this recipe by four.

A roux is an equal mixture of cooked flour and oil or butter that is added to soup as a flavoring and thickener. Traditionally, a roux is made by heating oil or butter in a skillet, over moderate heat, and adding flour while stirring constantly as the mixture develops a distinctive nutty flavor. The longer the roux is cooked the deeper the color and the more intense the flavor. Generally, a light brown roux is used with dark meats, a dark reddish-brown roux is used with light meats and seafood, and a charcoal-brown roux is best for gumbos.

BEST RESTAURANT BOSTON CLAM CHOWDER

Combine celery, onions, potatoes, clams, thyme, oregano, basil, bouillon, and pepper; cook 30 to 45 minutes until vegetables and potatoes are soft.

Melt butter and add flour and garlic, stir constantly until slightly brown. Combine with vegetable mixture and add half-and-half. Stir well and cook for 10 minutes.

Fred Calixtro
Hobee's Restaurant
1st Place Winner

 This recipe yields $4^1/_2$ gallons. Invite your family, friends, and neighbors and enjoy a big batch.

2 bunches celery, chopped

$1^1/_2$ pounds onions, chopped

6 pounds red potatoes, diced

6 32-ounce cans clams with juice

3 tablespoons dried thyme

1 tablespoon dried oregano

2 tablespoons dried basil

1 cup fish bouillon

2 tablespoons white pepper

3 pounds butter

6 cups flour

6 cloves fresh garlic, chopped

1 gallon of 2 percent milk

CHEF SAL'S MANHATTAN-STYLE CLAM CHOWDER

Roux

2 pounds margarine

1 pound flour

7 or 8 medium yellow onions, chopped

1 bunch of celery, chopped

1 16-ounce can clams

2 16-ounce cans clam juice

2 tablespoons clam base

2 2$\frac{1}{2}$-pound cans of stewed tomatoes, chopped

2 medium bell peppers, chopped

1$\frac{1}{2}$ gallons water

2 teaspoons ground rosemary or 1$\frac{1}{2}$ teaspoons rosemary stems

1 teaspoon white pepper

10 medium potatoes, peeled and cubed

To make roux, melt margarine and add flour a little at a time. Whip well.

Combine onions, celery, clams, clam juice, clam base, tomatoes, bell peppers, and water in a 2-gallon pot. Heat to boiling and cook until clams and vegetables are tender, 25 to 30 minutes. Add rosemary, pepper, and potatoes; cook for another 15 to 20 minutes or until potatoes are tender.

Thicken with roux, as needed, then simmer until thoroughly warm.

Chef Sal diNappoli
Santa Cruz, CA

COASTAL CHRISTMAS

HUMBOLDT COUNTY

Annual. Mid-November through New Year's Eve.

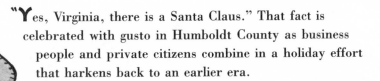

14

"Yes, Virginia, there is a Santa Claus." That fact is celebrated with gusto in Humboldt County as business people and private citizens combine in a holiday effort that harkens back to an earlier era.

Why suffer with holiday shopping when you can enjoy the holidays surrounded by redwood trees, Victorian architecture, fishing boats, and twinkling lights on water? A Coastal Christmas is hot buttered rum in front of cozy fireplaces, horse and carriage rides in Eureka's Old Town, and strolling choirs and carolers providing music and entertainment.

Dozens of outstanding seasonal activities take place in the communities of Eureka, Ferndale, Willow Creek, Arcata, Fortuna, Redway, Briceland, Orick, Bayside, and Benbow. The nice thing is, the close proximity of these small communities makes it possible to take in several holiday events during a weekend or mid-week getaway.

Although specific events vary annually, recent attendees have delighted in brunch with Santa; an afternoon tea featuring tasty scones; tea sandwiches; holiday cookies; and daily servings of locally caught, live, and just-cooked Dungeness crab. Other feastings include a taste of local foods and wines, ethnic holiday dinners, and the Redwood Cuisine and Crafts Fair.

If you can, plan several days to visit. A complimentary sixteen-page schedule of events for A Coastal Christmas is available from the Eureka/Humboldt County Convention and Visitors Bureau.

Humbolt County, situated about 200 miles north of San Francisco, contains a scenic 110-mile coastline, more than 160,000 acres of majestic redwoods, and an unspoiled terrain of valleys and rolling hills.

PÂTÉ DE FOIES DE VOLAILLE

Chicken Liver Pâté

1/4 cup butter

1/2 pound chicken livers, halved

3 ounces mushrooms, chopped

2 tablespoons chopped green onions or shallots

2 tablespoons chopped parsley

1/4 teaspoon crushed thyme

dash salt

1 tablespoon brandy

1/4 cup Madeira wine

1/2 cup butter, cut in pieces

1/2 can black olives, chopped

In frying pan over medium heat, melt 1/4 cup butter. Add chicken livers, mushrooms, green onions or shallots, parsley, thyme, a dash of salt and cook, stirring until livers are brown on all sides and well done. Warm brandy, pour over liver and ignite, shake pan until flame dies. Add wine, simmer briefly. Put liver mixture in blender and purée with butter, adding a few pieces at a time. If mixture seems a little too dry, add a little more wine. Blend until smooth. Remove from blender. Fold in the olives.

Pour into large tureen or small individual tureens and chill until firm, several hours or overnight. Keeps for 2 or 3 days if refrigerated and covered. Serve with crusty French bread or crackers.

Doug and Lily Vieyra
An Elegant Victorian Mansion Bed & Breakfast Inn
Eureka, CA

SWISS SCONES

Place flour, sugar, baking soda, baking powder, and salt in medium bowl and mix well. Cut butter into flour mixture with pastry cutter, until it resembles coarse cornmeal. Add raisins and orange peel. Add buttermilk and mix with fork until dough leaves sides of bowl. Place dough on floured board and pat into a circle or rectangle $1/2$ inch thick. Cut in 2-inch circles or hearts with a cookie cutter and place on lightly greased cookie sheet. Space about $1^1/_2$ inches apart. Brush tops with cream or milk and sprinkle with sugar/cinnamon mixture.

Bake at 425° for 12 to 14 minutes, until tops are lightly brown. Serve fresh from the oven or cool and place in airtight container. Can be stored 1 or 2 days, but are better fresh. Makes about a dozen scones. Variations: substitute dates for raisins or try chocolate chips.

Doug and Lily Vieyra
An Elegant Victorian Mansion Bed & Breakfast Inn
Eureka, CA

**Serve with scrambled eggs
or a bowl of fresh fruit.**

$1^1/_2$ cups flour

$1/_4$ cup sugar

$1/_4$ teaspoon baking soda

$1^1/_4$ teaspoons baking powder

$1/_4$ teaspoon salt

$3/_4$ cube butter, cold,
cut in small pieces

$1/_2$ cup golden raisins

grated peel of small orange

$1/_2$ cup buttermilk, or $1/_2$ cup milk
with 1 teaspoon of lemon juice

milk or cream to brush top of scones

2 teaspoons sugar mixed with
$1/_4$ teaspoon cinnamon

CHRISTMAS FAVORITE COCONUT-PECAN BARS

$^{1}/_{2}$ cup butter

$^{1}/_{2}$ cup sugar

1 cup flour

2 eggs

1 cup brown sugar

1 tablespoon flour

1 cup chopped pecans

$^{1}/_{2}$ cup flaked coconut

1 teaspoon vanilla

$^{1}/_{8}$ teaspoon salt

Mix butter, sugar, and flour. Press into 8x8-inch pan and bake at 350° for 19 to 20 minutes. While baking, combine remaining ingredients. Pour onto baked crust and bake 20 minutes more. Dust with powdered sugar, if desired. Cut while hot.

Ramone's Bakery and Cafe
Eureka, CA

CRANBERRY ORANGE MUFFINS

Sift together all dry ingredients. In separate bowl, mix all other ingredients and slowly add dry ingredients, blending. Bake in a 350° oven for 15 to 25 minutes. Makes 24 muffins.

Ramone's Bakery and Cafe
Eureka, CA

2 cups whole wheat flour

2½ cups white flour

⅔ cup brown sugar

⅔ cup sugar

2 tablespoons baking powder

1 teaspoon salt

2 cups milk

⅔ cup oil

2 eggs

1 ripe banana

2 cups chopped cranberries

grated peel of 2 oranges

DRY BEAN FESTIVAL
TRACY
Annual. First weekend in August.

Downtown Tracy is the location of the Dry Bean Festival. The two-day event is known for its quality entertainment, bean dishes, and good humor. Go ahead, soak up the sounds of music, the scents of festival foods, and the essence of the harvest season.

Stop by the Bean Pavilion and you'll discover plenty of savory bean cuisine from local restaurants and corporate sponsors. Bean research, recipes, celebrity chef demonstrations, and even a chili bean cook-off add flavor to the event.

Walk along Bean Boulevard and Lima Lane to discover nearly one hundred booths selling arts, crafts, antiques, collectibles, and more bean souvenirs than you ever thought possible. After all, couldn't you use another bean pot?

Kids of all ages love meeting the festival's friendly and humorous mascots, Pinto and Cookie Bean. Bring the camera; it's a fun photo opportunity the entire family will cherish. Pony rides, petting zoo, and a tractor pull are available for youngsters. Also on hand are the Bean Run, classic and antique cars, plenty of lively entertainment, and some of the country's very best bean cuisine.

To top it all off, you'll be able to proudly tell your friends you've experienced what is currently America's only festival celebrating and honoring the dry bean.

All recipes in this section were contributed by the Dry Bean Festival.

LIMAS CON CHILE Y QUESO

Soak and cook the dry limas according to package directions. Drain while hot, saving cooking liquid, adding water if needed to make $1\frac{1}{2}$ cups. Spread $\frac{1}{3}$ limas in shallow $2\frac{1}{2}$-quart casserole. Sprinkle with half of each herb. Tear each chili lengthwise, seed, and cut crosswise in $\frac{1}{2}$-inch strips. Cut cheese in strips $\frac{1}{4}$ inch thick by 1 inch wide. Layer half the chilies and $\frac{1}{3}$ of cheese over beans. Repeat process for second layer. Top with remaining beans and cheese. Stir bean liquid into sour cream until smooth. Salt to taste. Pour over beans.

Bake uncovered at 325° for 30 to 40 minutes until bubbling throughout. Just before serving, garnish with parsley, spoonfuls of additional sour cream, and paprika.

1 pound dry large limas

$\frac{1}{4}$ teaspoon basil or thyme

$\frac{1}{8}$ teaspoon oregano

2 4-ounce cans whole green chilies (mild)

$\frac{1}{2}$ pound Monterey Jack cheese

$\frac{3}{4}$ cup sour cream

chopped parsley, sour cream, and paprika for garnish

PLANTATION BLACKEYES

1 pound dry blackeyes

1/4 pound bacon

1 cup chopped onions

2 cups canned whole tomatoes

1 1/2 cups water

2 teaspoons salt

1/4 teaspoon pepper

3/4 teaspoon oregano

1/2 teaspoon thyme

1/2 teaspoon rosemary

1 1/2 cups grated cheddar cheese

Wash, sort, and soak blackeyes as directed on package. Cut bacon into 1-inch pieces. Cook bacon in Dutch oven or heavy pot until fat is rendered. Add onions, and cook until tender. Add tomatoes with their liquid, breaking them up with a spoon. Add water, seasonings, and soaked, drained blackeyes. Simmer, covered, until beans are just tender (about 30 minutes).

Stir in cheese, pour mixture into a 3-quart rectangular casserole, and bake uncovered 30 to 40 minutes at 375°. Serve this as a dinner entrée or a one-dish supper.

 These blackeyes go great with cornbread.

SNAPPY BEAN DIP

Place drained beans and remaining ingredients, except 1 tablespoon of the green onions, in blender container. Blend until smooth. Or, mash beans to purée and mix with remaining ingredients. Place in small bowl and garnish with the remaining tablespoon chopped green onion. Serve as a dip with crisp raw vegetables or chips.

 For a tasty open-faced sandwich, spread this dip over buttered bread, sprinkle with cheddar cheese, and broil until cheese melts.

1²/₃ cup drained pink beans, cooked (or 1 16-ounce can)

2 tablespoons mayonnaise

1 teaspoon Worcestershire sauce

1 teaspoon chopped and seeded canned jalapeño peppers

³/₄ teaspoon salt

3 tablespoons chopped green onion

PORTUGUESE-STYLE BEAN SOUP

1 to 1$\frac{1}{2}$ pounds ham hock

2 onions, sliced

1 stalk celery, coarsely cut

1 bay leaf

3$\frac{1}{3}$ cups drained kidney beans,
cooked or canned (2 16-ounce cans)

6 ounces pepperoni
sliced $\frac{1}{4}$ inch thick

2 potatoes, diced

1 carrot, diced

1 turnip, diced

1 small cabbage, sliced

1 8-ounce can tomato sauce

2 teaspoons salt

Simmer ham hock, half of the onion, celery, and bay leaf in 1 to 1$\frac{1}{2}$ quarts of water for 1 hour. Strain, reserving stock and ham. Bone ham, cut into $\frac{1}{2}$-inch cubes. Add all ingredients to stock, simmer 1$\frac{1}{2}$ hours or until vegetables are tender.

 This soup freezes well.

EGGPLANT FESTIVAL

LOOMIS

Annual. Third Saturday in September.

16

The Eggplant Festival started several years ago when three Loomis residents decided the community needed an event that was interesting, fun, and celebrated the area's farming industry.

Bring on the eggplants! Discover an exciting line-up of fun events each year as the Loomis Eggplant Festival brings plenty of food, lots of fun, an abundance of good competitions, and enough eggplant recipes to publish its own official *Eggplant Cookbook.* The cookbook is available at the festival or may be obtained by mail.

There is plenty to do other than eating eggplant delicacies. Kids can create sculptures made of eggplants; Mr. Eggplant greets visitors; the high school Golden Eagle Marching Band performs during the parade; and there is always the "Egganapolis 500," where decorated eggplants are raced down a wooden plank in small wagons. The "race" in itself might give you reason to attend this delightful and amusing community event.

Just off Interstate 80, the small town of Loomis is one of the state's important fruit-and-vegetable producing centers. The area is dotted with dozens of groves, fields, ranches, packing sheds, and produce markets. Free shuttle bus service is provided to the festival from the Del Oro High School parking lot.

EGGPLANT STRUDEL

1 medium eggplant, diced

$^1/_2$ teaspooon salt

1 cup sugar

1 tablespoon cinnamon

1 tablespoon lemon juice

1 cup sour cream

$^3/_4$ cup raisins

$^3/_4$ cup chopped walnuts

Pastry Dough

1 package phyllo dough

$^1/_2$ stick (4 tablespoons) butter, melted

Cinnamon Syrup

$^1/_2$ cup sugar

1 tablespoon butter

1 tablespoon cinnamon

1 tablespoon water

Combine eggplant, salt, sugar, cinnamon, and lemon juice. Chill 15 minutes. Stir in sour cream, raisins, and walnuts and set aside. Lay out several layers of dough and brush top with a layer of butter, using a pastry brush. Spoon eggplant mixture in a line along one side of the dough.

Roll dough carefully around the mixture shaped in a long tube. Cut slits across the top. Bake at 350° for 35 to 40 minutes. Use a pan beneath the strudel to catch the drippings. Over low heat, stir sugar, cinnamon, butter and water to make a syrup. Cook 10 minutes. Remove strudel from oven to cool and then pour syrup over the top.

Julie Beasley
Grand Sweepstakes Award Winner

NEW LOOMIS EGGPLANT SALAD

Roast eggplant on barbeque until soft and skin is charred on all sides. Cool, then peel and dice. Add to a large bowl which has been rubbed with garlic. Add remaining vegetables one at a time, stirring after each addition. Squeeze in lemon juice, oil, salt, and pepper. Serve at room temperature on romaine leaves.

Michael Brigandi
1st Place Winner, Side Dish Competition

2 large eggplants

4 to 8 garlic cloves, minced

1 large green pepper, seeded, diced

1 medium red onion, diced

1 large cucumber,
peeled, seeded, diced

2 large tomatoes,
peeled, seeded, diced,

juice of 1 lemon

3 or 4 tablespoons fruity olive oil

salt and pepper to taste

romaine leaves

XIM XIM EGGPLANT

2½ tablespoons dried salted shrimp

½ cup dry-roasted peanuts

¼ cup olive oil

1 medium eggplant cut in
1½ - to 2-inch pieces

1 tablespoon minced garlic

½ cup minced white onions

2 13.5 cans coconut milk

salt and pepper to taste

1 tablespoon chili pepper

1 tablespoon paprika

3 tablespoons chopped cilantro

fresh cilantro sprigs for garnish

lime wedges for garnish

¼ cup whole dry-roasted peanuts

Grind ½ cup dry roasted peanuts with the shrimp in a blender or food processor until well combined. Set aside. Heat oil in a large skillet over medium heat. Fry eggplant until slightly translucent. Remove and let cool. Remove all but 1 tablespoon of oil from skillet, then sauté garlic and onion until translucent. Add eggplant to onion and garlic mix, then add the coconut milk, followed with ground shrimp and peanuts.

Heat until lightly boiling, stirring until thickened. Lower heat and add salt and pepper, then the chili pepper, paprika, and cilantro. Serve over bed of steamed rice. Garnish with cilantro sprigs, lemon wedges, and whole peanuts.

Pamela Brigandi
1st Place Winner, Appetizer Competition

 Xim xim is pronounced sheen sheen.

EASY EGGPLANT PARMESAN

Cook eggplant in oil with garlic in large skillet over medium-high heat; set aside. Combine bread crumbs with 2 tablespoons Parmesan cheese. Place eggplant slices in 13x9-inch glass casserole, overlapping slices if necessary. Sprinkle with bread crumb mixture. Combine rice, sauce, and remaining Parmesan cheese in large bowl; pour mixture over eggplant. Sprinkle with mozzarella cheese. Bake at 375° for 20 minutes or until cheese is melted and lightly browned.

U.S.A. Rice Council
Houston, TX

2 medium eggplants, peeled and sliced $1/2$ inch thick

2 tablespoons vegetable oil

1 clove garlic, minced

$2/3$ cup Italian-style bread crumbs

$3/4$ cup Parmesan cheese

3 cups cooked rice

1 30-ounce jar prepared spaghetti sauce

2 cups shredded mozzarella cheese

FESTA ITALIANA

SACRAMENTO

Annual. First weekend in August.

Life's pleasures shouldn't be denied. Festa Italiana is an extravaganza of food, entertainment, culture, and Italian-style fun. Best of all, dozens of chefs from local Italian restaurants bring extravagant entries and sinfully rich desserts. You'll find yourself awash in the captivating aroma of fresh rosemary, basil, garlic, and tomato sauce. And the smell lives up to its promise with a delicious array of Italian specialties.

Italian cooks from throughout California come to the event and show off traditional favorites including pasta, foccacia and sausage sandwiches, polenta, pesole, canolli, and many other treats. Italian wines and other beverages are available during the festival.

You'll revel in the summertime splendor of this event. The celebration includes live entertainment, music, dancing, a children's area, games, an Italian Marketplace and art fair, and an Italian car show.

California's Capitol is located in Sacramento. The city's history began in 1839 when Johann Augustus Sutter settled at the confluence of the American and Sacramento rivers. Gold was discovered in 1848, just thirty miles east of the city. California became a state in 1850, and Sacramento its capital four years later.

You may not discover gold at Festa Italiana, but you're guaranteed some of the finest and most flavorful Italian food found around this neck of the woods.

RICOTTA SFINGI

Traditional Dessert

Cream ricotta and sugar until smooth. Add eggs, one at a time, while continuing to beat. Add flour and baking powder. Beat until smooth. Drop spoonfuls into hot oil. Fry until light golden brown. When done, remove with a slotted spoon and place to drain on paper towels. Let cool a little and sprinkle heavily with powdered sugar.

Italian Cultural Society
Sacramento, CA

$1^1/_2$ pounds ricotta

4 tablespoons sugar

4 eggs

2 cups flour

4 tablespoons baking powder

oil for frying (olive or canola is best)

powdered sugar

PENNE AL SALAMI

1 pound penne (dry pasta)

2 tablespoons olive oil

2 tablespoons butter

1 sprig rosemary

a few sage leaves

$1/2$ pound salami, cut into thin strips

$1/2$ cup dry white wine

2 eggs

$1/4$ to $1/2$ cup grated Parmesan cheese

salt and pepper to taste

Heat the oil, butter, rosemary, and sage in a small pan; add the salami. Cook for a few minutes and then add the wine. Let the wine evaporate and then lower the cooking temperature. In a bowl, beat the eggs, Parmesan cheese, and a touch of salt and pepper. Cook the penne al dente and drain. Place in a bowl with the egg mixture and mix well. Remove the rosemary and the sage. Pour the salami sauce over the penne and serve hot with plenty of grated Parmesan cheese.

Italian Cultural Society
Sacramento, CA

SAVORY SPAGHETTI SAUCE

Peel and mince garlic. Cook garlic and onions in oil until tender. Add water and put in the rest of the ingredients, except for mushrooms. Bring to a boil, then simmer for 1 to 1¹/₂ hours. Add undrained mushrooms and simmer an additional 20 minutes and serve.

Family Travel Log
Recipes From Across the United States
Kewanee, IL

Make a large batch of this sauce and freeze any leftover for use at a later date.

2 cloves garlic

1 large onion

2 tablespoons cooking oil

1 cup water

6 medium tomatoes

1 16-ounce can tomato paste

¹/₈ teaspoon pepper

2 teaspoons beef granules

1 tablespoon sugar

¹/₂ teaspoon salt

¹/₂ teaspoon dried basil

1 bay leaf

1 4-ounce can mushrooms

FESTIVAL OF GOAT CHEESE
& NORTH COAST WINE
SONOMA COUNTY
Annual. Dates vary.

18

Whether or not you're presently a goat cheese enthusiast, you don't want to miss the premier goat cheese event of the year. It's here you'll discover several California goat cheese producers offering samples of their cheeses. Simultaneously, professional chefs prepare signature dishes and you're able to taste their culinary creations. Throughout the event, wineries from Sonoma, Napa, and Mendocino counties pour their wine and offer tastings.

Held in the evening, the festival includes live jazz and a fun, professionally judged culinary competition. Awards are given for the "Queen of the Goats" and "People's Choice."

Each year, the Festival of Goat Cheese & North Coast Wine is held at a different location within Sonoma County, but plenty of flavorful food, award-winning wine, and fine entertainment continues wherever the event takes place. The festivity is sponsored by the Redwood Dairy Goat Association and proceeds provide educational workshops and seminars.

Sonoma County is located about an hour north of San Francisco. Its restive atmosphere will make you forget all about hectic and overcrowded city life.

JALAPEÑO RELLENO

Filling the Jalapeños: Cream together 2 eggs and Chèvre; add green onion and cilantro. Mix in lime juice, salt and pepper to taste. Fill each half of jalapeño with cheese mixture. Put one half on top of other half of jalapeño and press together. Refrigerate at least six hours.

Breading the Jalapeño Relleno: Set up breading station with a bowl of flour, a bowl of egg wash made with milk and 2 eggs blended, and a bowl with the bread crumbs and corn flake crumbs mixed together. Dredge a chilled jalapeño in flour, then drop it in the egg wash bowl. Continue this process until all the jalapeños are in the egg wash. Drain the jalapeños. Dredge them in bread crumb-corn flake mixture and immediately place on waxed paper.

Cooking the Jalapeño Relleno: Jalapeños are ready to deep-fry at 350° at this point, or they can be wrapped and stored in freezer. They can be deep-fried with excellent results from the frozen state.

Chef John Meidinger
Tides Wharf Restaurant
Bodega Bay, CA

4 eggs

8 ounces Chèvre Fresca, Fromage Blanc, or other soft, full-bodied cheese

$1/2$ tablespoon minced green onions

1 tablespoon chopped cilantro

1 tablespoon lime juice

salt and white pepper

12 jalapeño peppers, halved and seeded

$1\frac{1}{2}$ cups flour

1 cup milk

$1/2$ cup bread crumbs

$1/2$ cup corn flake crumbs

ANISE & BODEGA GOAT CHEESE ON BABY BOK CHOY

1 teaspoon minced garlic

2 tablespoons peanut oil

$\frac{1}{2}$ teaspoon sesame oil

$\frac{1}{2}$ pound fresh shiitake mushrooms

4 ounces cream from Bodega goat cheese

4 kernels anise, crushed to fine powder

24 fresh baby bok choy leaves (or other greens)

Sauté garlic in peanut and sesame oil for 1 minute. Add thin slices of shiitake. Sauté 3 more minutes. Add small bits of cheese, sprinkle with anise, and stir quickly. Immediately remove from heat and place spoonfuls on crisp bok choy leaves and serve.

Chef Barbara Hom
Night Owl Catering
Sebastopol, CA

GRILLED SMOKED TURKEY WITH CHÈVRE CHEDDAR ON BLACK BREAD

Mix softened butter, tomato, sage, honey, and pepper. On the bottom slice of bread, spread thin layer of the butter mixture. Top with cheese. Layer with the smoked turkey, then the arugula, then onions, and more cheese. Spread the inside of the top bread slice with a thin layer of butter. Butter outsides of sandwich. Then grill in a hot frying pan on both sides until browned.

Chef Andy Gold
Carter House
Eureka, CA

Butter mixture

$^1/_2$ pound sweet butter, softened

1 tomato, skinned, seeded, finely chopped, and drained

$^1/_4$ cup fresh sage

3 tablespoons honey

black pepper to taste

12 slices black bread

1 pound Chèvre cheddar, thinly sliced or grated

$^3/_4$ pound smoked turkey breast, sliced thinly

2 bunches arugula, washed and dried

1 large red onion, sliced thin

FISH FEED AND ART FESTIVAL

TRINIDAD

Annual. June weekend varies.

19

What would you expect from a fishing village filled with artists? A celebration that honors both the fishing industry and the art community, that's what. It's a weekend to feast on salmon and white fish as dinners are served throughout the weekend and artists and crafters exhibit and sell their wares. The barbecued salmon and deep-fried whitefish dinners include all the trimmings, and homemade desserts are available to top off your meal. Throughout the event, musicians, dancers, clowns, and the children's choir entertain and perform to the delight of all festival goers.

You'll probably want to walk off some of the feast, and you can do just that by taking a tour of the Trinidad Head Lighthouse, opened only once a year, during the festival. If you don't feel like walking, there's a shuttle from town that takes you out to the Coast Guard Station.

It may not be the West Indies, but California's Trinidad is certainly a community of fishing enthusiasts, artists, photographers, food, and friendliness. It's located along the coast about 285 miles north of San Francisco and 80 miles from the Oregon border. This little fishing village welcomes visitors to walk along its sandy beaches, or hike one of the most spectacular vista walks on the entire coast of California.

SMOKED SALMON MOUSSE

Sauté shallots in butter until golden. Add fish, mix, and remove from heat. Place in blender, add cream cheese, sour cream, butter, and blend well. Add lemon juice and vodka. Blend until smooth. Remove mixture to bowl and fold in the whipped cream. Refrigerate for a couple of hours or up to 2 days. Serve cold, but not too chilled, on crackers or warm French bread.

Doug and Lily Vieyra
An Elegant Victorian Mansion Bed & Breakfast Inn
Eureka, CA

2 tablespoons unsalted butter

1 tablespoon finely chopped shallots
or green onions

2 to 3 ounces smoked salmon,
boned and flaked

$1/4$ cup cream cheese

$1/4$ sour cream

$1/4$ cup unsalted butter softened

2 tablespoons lemon juice

1 tablespoon vodka

$1/4$ cup whipping cream, whipped

SURIMI SEAFOOD–ZUCCHINI FRITTATA WITH FRESH TOMATO SAUCE

2 tablespoons vegetable oil

1 zucchini, thinly sliced

1/2 cup chopped onion

1/4 cup chopped green pepper

3 eggs

6 egg whites

2 teaspoons finely chopped fresh basil, or 1/2 teaspoon dried basil

1/2 teaspoon salt, optional

1/4 teaspoon pepper

6 ounces crab or lobster-flavored surimi seafood, chunk style

2 tablespoons butter or margarine

3 cups tomato sauce

Preheat oven to 375°. Heat oil in 10-inch, ovenproof, heavy metal skillet over medium heat. Add zucchini, onion, and green pepper; cook 5 minutes, stirring often. Place in mixing bowl and set aside to cool slightly. In second mixing bowl, beat eggs and egg whites with basil, salt, and pepper until well blended. Add zucchini mixture and surimi seafood, beat well.

Meanwhile, melt butter in same skillet over medium heat, swirling skillet to coat evenly with butter. Pour in egg–surimi seafood mixture and place skillet on middle shelf of oven. Bake 12 to 15 minutes, or until eggs are set throughout. Loosen around edges with metal spatula and cut into wedges. Serve hot with 1/2 cup tomato sauce over each frittata slice.

Surimi Seafood Education Center
Arlington, VA

Surimi seafood is a crab look-alike product which adds flavor to dishes from around the world.

CALIFORNIA CIOPPINO

In a large, heavy stockpot, heat oil and sauté garlic, onion, celery tops, red pepper flakes, and parsley until onion is transparent and vegetables are limp (do not allow to burn). Add wine, tomatoes, bay leaf, oregano, and basil. Bring to a boil, lower heat, and simmer covered for 20 minutes. Add seafood to broth, beginning with varieties needing longer cooking time.

When shrimp turn pink and opaque, clam and mussel shells open, and fish flakes easily (approximately 20 minutes), remove from heat and ladle into soup bowls. Garnish with parsley and lemon wedges, if desired.

California Seafood Council
Santa Barbara, CA

$1/4$ cup olive oil

3 cloves minced garlic

1 large onion, chopped

$1/2$ cup chopped celery tops

$1/4$ teaspoon red pepper flakes

$1/2$ cup chopped parsley

2 cups wine or chicken stock

2 cups chopped tomatoes

1 bay leaf

1 teaspoon chopped fresh oregano

1 teaspoon chopped fresh basil

2 to 3 pounds California seafood (the seafood assortment may include California shrimp, crab, spiny lobster, clams, mussels, rockfish, and halibut)

parsley and lemon for granish

GARLIC FESTIVAL

GILROY

Annual. Last full weekend in July. *20*

So much garlic is grown in Gilroy that humorist Will Rogers once exclaimed, "It's the only town in America where you can marinate a steak just by hanging it out on the clothesline."

The plant that's affectionately nicknamed the "Stinking Rose" is celebrated at the Gilroy Garlic Festival. This event includes fine wine and entertainment, tennis and golf tournaments, a children's area, arts and crafts, a garlic recipe contest, and Gourmet Alley.

Gourmet Alley is the spectacular culinary heart of the Garlic Festival. Here, in a gigantic kitchen area, you'll discover local chefs performing magic over blazing fire pits to the delight of spectators. Throughout the celebration, chefs keep iron skillets the size of bicycle wheels sizzling.

An army of volunteers helps chefs barbecue huge chunks of sirloin and gently sauté bright red and green peppers for the popular pepper steak sandwiches. Other garlic-laced delicacies include stir-fried vegetables, scampi, pasta con pesto, stuffed mushrooms with garlic, mountains of garlic bread, and a scrumptious red sauce with pasta. Be sure you save room for some of the festival's garlic ice cream.

This three-day festival is a fun-lover's delight and a garlic aficionado's paradise. You'll become such a fan of the "Stinking Rose" you'll want to pick up a copy of several garlic lover's cookbooks available at the festival.

Gilroy is 30 miles south of San Jose on U.S. Highway 101 and 30 miles north of Monterey. The festival is held at Christmas Hill Park at the southwest edge of town.

FORTY-CLOVE CHICKEN FILICE

Place chicken pieces into shallow baking pan, skin side up. Sprinkle all ingredients evenly over top of chicken. Squeeze juice from lemon and pour over top. Cut lemon rind into pieces and arrange throughout chicken. Cover with foil and bake at 375° for 40 minutes. Remove foil and bake an additional 15 minutes. Salt and pepper to taste.

Val Filice, contributor
Gilroy Garlic Festival Association
Gilroy, CA

1 frying chicken, cut in pieces

40 cloves fresh garlic

$^1/_2$ cup dry white wine

$^1/_4$ cup dry vermouth

$^1/_4$ cup olive oil

4 stalks celery, cut in 1-inch pieces

1 teaspoon oregano

2 teaspoons dry basil

6 sprigs minced parsley

pinch of crushed red pepper

1 lemon

salt and pepper to taste

GARLIC BUTTER

6 cloves garlic

1 cup butter

Add mashed garlic cloves or the equivalent in dehydrated or processed garlic to suit your taste to sticks of butter (about 6 cloves fresh garlic per stick is recommended). If you wish, add a few herbs and salt lightly. Form into logs, wrap in plastic, and freeze. Slice off as needed.

Gilroy Garlic Festival Association
Gilroy, CA

Make logs of garlic butter and freeze them to have on hand to melt on broiled meats, mix into fresh cooked vegetables, or spread on bread.

BETTY JAYNE'S GARLIC SOUP WITH CHEESE BREAD

In saucepan, heat oil over medium heat. Add garlic and sauté until soft and golden. Add chicken broth, water, beans, salt, pepper, bay leaves, and jalapeño pepper. Simmer 5 minutes. Pour into blender and purée. Return to saucepan. Stir in cream and heat through. Toast bread lightly. Sprinkle with Parmesan cheese and broil 3 minutes or until cheese is golden and bubbly. Serve toast in soup.

Betty Jayne Jones, contributor
Gilroy Garlic Festival Association
Gilroy, CA

4 teaspoons olive oil

30 chopped garlic cloves

1 quart chicken broth

2 cups water

2 15-ounce cans canellini beans

1 teaspoon each salt and pepper

2 bay leaves

1 fresh jalapeño pepper, seeded, chopped

1 cup whipping cream

12 slices French bread

Parmesan cheese, grated

EGGPLANT ANTIPASTA

4 eggplants (Chinese or Japanese)

4 tomatoes, chopped

1 bulb garlic, peeled and crushed or finely chopped

finely chopped fresh basil

Parmesan cheese, grated (optional)

olive oil

salt and pepper to taste

Cut eggplant in half, lengthwise, then again crosswise so you end up with 4 pieces per eggplant. Make a couple of slits on the meat of the eggplant without cutting through to the skin. Stuff chopped tomatoes into the slits of the eggplant, place garlic on top and sprinkle with basil. Sprinkle with Parmesan cheese, if desired. Drizzle with a lot of olive oil. Bake in a pan at 350° for 25 to 30 minutes. Salt and pepper to taste.

Rudy and Gloria Melone, contributors
Gilroy Garlic Festival Association
Gilroy, CA

GRAPE STOMP

MURPHYS

Annual. Date varies with the harvest.

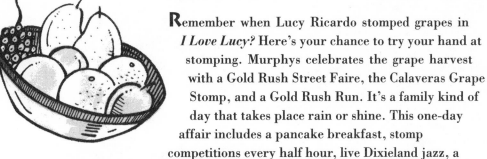

Remember when Lucy Ricardo stomped grapes in *I Love Lucy?* Here's your chance to try your hand at stomping. Murphys celebrates the grape harvest with a Gold Rush Street Faire, the Calaveras Grape Stomp, and a Gold Rush Run. It's a family kind of day that takes place rain or shine. This one-day affair includes a pancake breakfast, stomp competitions every half hour, live Dixieland jazz, a silent auction, a costume contest, fine eats, winemaking displays, and wine tasting from all seven Calaveras County wineries.

The stomping involves teams of two participants—one stomper and one swabber who collects the juice. The teams stomp twenty-five pounds of grapes for three minutes. The team that collects the most juice wins the heat and is eligible for the finals. Cash prizes and awards are given to the first and second place teams. If you want to register to participate in the Grape Stomp, it's best to do it well in advance of the event in order to guarantee your participation.

Established in 1848, the town of Murphys hit a population of 1,200 during the days of gold digging and hard living. Today, Murphys has a population of about 2,300, several wineries, the famous historic Murphys Hotel, and some of the friendliest people around.

From California Highway 49 in Angels Camp, follow scenic California Highway 4 east exactly 9 miles to the historic village of Murphys. Be sure to allow plenty of time to enjoy the many nooks and crannies in this charming community.

SAUVIGNON MUSHROOMS

4 cloves garlic, crushed

3 tablespoons olive oil

¼ cup Sauvignon Blanc

¼ teaspoon almond extract

1 tablespoon Worcestershire sauce

1 tablespoon lemon juice

1 tablespoon chopped parsley

¼ cup sliced almonds

1 pound small fresh mushrooms

salt to taste

Combine all ingredients except mushrooms in a skillet and simmer 10 minutes. Add mushrooms and simmer an additional 10 minutes. Salt to taste.

Cynthia Gomes
Tasting Room Manager, Stevenot Winery
Author, All American Sports Fan Cookbook
Murphys, CA

This gourmet delight is great over beef, lamb, or chicken.

MARINATED CHUCK ROAST

Make about 10 slits in roast and insert garlic halves. Mix marinade and marinate meat overnight in a covered container. Keep refrigerated until ready to barbecue and grill as desired. Use extra marinade to baste.

Cynthia Gomes
Tasting Room Manager, Stevenot Winery
Author, *All American Sports Fan Cookbook*
Murphys, CA

3 to 4 pounds chuck roast

4 to 5 cloves garlic,
peeled and halved

<u>Marinade</u>
1 cup Cabernet wine

$\frac{1}{2}$ teaspoon Cajun seasoning

$\frac{1}{4}$ cup sugar

1 teaspoon nutmeg or to taste

$\frac{1}{2}$ teaspoon salt

juice of 1 orange

GRILLED DUCK BREAST WITH CHERRY SAUCE

4 duck breasts

2 teaspoons olive oil

1 teaspoon chopped fresh thyme

salt and pepper

Cherry Sauce

$1/4$ cup dried cherries

$1/4$ cup Kautz Ironstone Vineyards Merlot

2 teaspoons shallots

2 tablespoons balsamic vinegar

$1/4$ cup chicken stock

2 tablespoons butter

Remove skin from duck breasts. Toss duck breasts in olive oil, thyme, salt and pepper. Grill duck to medium.

To make cherry sauce, soak cherries in half of the Merlot for 20 minutes. Sauté shallots, add cherries, vinegar, and remaining Merlot. Add chicken stock, reduce to $1/4$ cup. Swirl in butter, pour over sliced duck breasts.

Kautz Ironstone Vineyards
Murphys, CA

ROAST LOIN OF LAMB

In a food processor, purée garlic, onion, and rosemary. Add Cabernet Franc and balsamic vinegar. Pour over loins of lamb. Marinate overnight or up to 3 days. Grill to medium-rare. Toss shiitake mushrooms in olive oil, salt and pepper to taste; grill. Slice loins of lamb and top with grilled mushrooms.

Kautz Ironstone Vineyards
Murphys, CA

 This recipe goes perfectly with Kautz Ironstone Vineyards' sumptuous Cabernet Franc.

2 cloves garlic

1 small onion, chopped

1 tablespoon rosemary, chopped

1 cup Kautz Ironstone Vineyards Cabernet Franc

$1/8$ teaspoon balsamic vinegar

4 loins of lamb

$1/4$ cup olive oil

$1/2$ pound shiitake mushrooms

salt and pepper

GRECIAN FESTIVAL

NOVATO COUNTY

Annual. Memorial Day weekend.

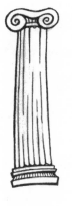

For more than twenty-five years, the weekend Grecian Festival has celebrated all things Greek. The festival takes place in a Grecian village setting at the Nativity of Christ Greek Orthodox Church in Novato. The site boasts a basilica-style Greek church and bell tower.

The festival offers exotic Greek food, pastries, imports, cultural exhibits, lectures, and tours to more than six thousand Greek enthusiasts annually. Children discover special things of interest during the weekend of traditional dress and dance. Gourmands look with longing and taste with awe during Greek cooking demonstrations. Everyone will enjoy live bouzouki band music. Put on your dancin' shoes and join the crowd during lessons given by award-winning dancers and dance troupes.

You'll be able to prepare your own Greek specialties after the dazzling food demonstrations and by picking up a copy of the festival's popular cookbook, *Greek Cookery Marin.* More than twelve thousand copies have been sold. They're available at the festival or year-round by writing to the festival.

The recipes in this section were all contributed by the Grecian Festival.

DOLOMATHES YIALANDJI

Stuffed Grape Leaves

Place onions in a large saucepan, add a little water to cover, and steam for about 10 minutes. Remove from heat and add salt, $1/2$ cup of the oil, mint, dill, scallions, and parsley. Stir and then add raw rice and juice of 2 lemons and mix well. Wash grape leaves thoroughly to remove all brine and cut stem ends.

Place 1 tablespoon of filling on ribbed-side of grape leaf. Starting at the base, fold over the sides and then roll to the end tip. Lay some grape leaves on bottom of Dutch oven or large saucepan and place stuffed leaves on top, putting them close together, seam side down, so they will not unravel. Arrange in layers until all are used. Pour hot water, remaining oil, and additional lemon juice over dolomathes and press down with heavy plate that is 1 inch smaller in circumference than the saucepan. This holds the dolomathes down during cooking. Cover saucepan and simmer for 30 to 45 minutes until rice is done. Serve cold with more lemon juice, if desired.

4 medium onions, chopped

1 teaspoon salt

1 cup olive oil

2 teaspoons chopped mint

1 teaspoon dill

6 bunches scallions, chopped
with part of green tops

$3/4$ cup finely chopped parsley

$2/3$ cup raw rice

1 12-ounce jar grape leaves

juice of 2 lemons

1 cup boiling water

additional lemon juice

SOUVLAKI

Barbecued Kebab

Marinade

1 cup olive oil

2 cloves garlic, mashed

salt and pepper to taste

juice of 2 lemons

1 cup red wine

2 pounds lamb or lean beef,
cubed or cut into strips

wooden skewers

Pilaf

1 cup rice

$\frac{1}{2}$ stick butter

1 lemon, more if desired

2 cups hot chicken broth

$\frac{1}{2}$ teaspoon salt

Make marinade with oil, garlic, salt, pepper, lemon juice, and red wine. Pour over meat and marinate overnight. Soak wooden skewers in water for at least 1 hour to prevent them from burning. Skewer meat and cook over charcoal until just pink inside. Baste frequently with marinade.

For pilaf, brown rice in butter, add lemon juice. When color changes, add chicken broth and salt. Cover and cook over low heat for about 30 minutes.

Serve kebabs with pilaf and salad.

TIROPETES

Cheese Puffs

Crumble feta cheese, add cottage cheese, and mix well. Beat eggs well and add cheeses. Stir in parsley. Melt butter over low heat and keep warm throughout procedure. Cut phyllo into strips, approximately 4x10 inches and set aside all but about $\frac{1}{5}$. Cover phyllo you are not using with plastic or wax paper and then a damp cloth. This prevents it from drying out.

Take top sheet from working stack. Set on work surface and brush well with melted butter. Fold each side lengthwise and brush with butter again. Place one teaspoon cheese mixture in bottom right corner of strip and fold over into a triangle. With each fold, be sure bottom edge is parallel with side edge as you progress. Brush finished puff lightly with butter and place on buttered baking sheet with sides. Take second sheet from stack and repeat until all cheese and filo are used. Bake puffs in 400° oven for about 15 to 20 minutes, or until light brown. Serve warm.

1 pound feta cheese

1 pound cottage cheese or ricotta

5 eggs

$\frac{1}{2}$ cup finely chopped parsley

$\frac{1}{2}$ to 1 pound butter, melted

1 pound phyllo pastry

HISTORIC CHRISTMAS BED & BREAKFAST TOUR

CALAVERAS COUNTY

Annual. Second Sunday in December.

23

If the holidays make you a little crazy, you'll find some much needed solace in Calaveras County. Ten dazzling and diverse historic hotels and bed-and-breakfast inns join forces and open their doors to the public for holiday viewing and delicious food and wine tasting during the Christmas season. This Calaveras County annual tour gives you a chance to enjoy flickering candlelight, the scent of pine trees, and tables laden with holiday food.

The participating lodgings include **Courtyard Bed & Breakfast Inn** (San Andreas), **Avery Hotel** (Avery), **Cooper House Bed & Breakfast Inn** (Angels Camp), **Dunbar House Bed & Breakfast Inn**, (Murphys), **Lodge at Manuel Mill** (Arnold), **Dorrington Hotel** (Dorrington), **Murphys Historic Hotel & Lodge** (Murphys), **The Redbud Inn** (Murphys), **Yellow Dog Inn** (Arnold), and **Robin's Nest** (San Andreas).

For the price of a commemorative wineglass or mug, you'll enjoy a magical afternoon of festive decorations, seasonal entertainment, and pleasurable appetizers. Tastings are poured by several wineries and the local microbrewery.

Calaveras County is located in the Mother Lode Country midway between San Francisco, Yosemite National Park, and Lake Tahoe. It's a region that still reflects the California Gold Rush era.

FOCACCIA

Knead together dough, 6 tablespoons olive oil, and rosemary. Press dough onto a 12x18-inch cookie sheet. Rub with 1 tablespoon olive oil. Sprinkle with $1/2$ cup Parmesan cheese and press lightly into dough. Let rise for 20 or 30 minutes. Bake at 375° for 20 minutes. Sprinkle $1/4$ cup Parmesan over bread and drizzle with 1 tablespoon olive oil. Top with rosemary sprigs. Bake additional 5 to 10 minutes until browned. Cut into squares.

Cooper House Bed and Breakfast
Angels Camp, CA

2 pounds frozen bread dough, thawed

8 tablespoons olive oil

2 tablespoons minced fresh rosemary, or 1 teaspoon dried

$3/4$ cup Parmesan cheese

rosemary sprigs

MARINATED MUSHROOMS

50 to 60 mushrooms

Marinade

$1/2$ cup olive oil

$1/2$ cup white wine vinegar

2 cloves garlic, crushed

1 teaspoon salt

1 teaspoon oregano

1 teaspoon crushed red pepper

Clean and boil mushrooms for 5 minutes. Drain well. Mix marinade ingredients. Store mushrooms in marinade indefinitely.

Lucy Thein, Innkeeper
The Courtyard Bed and Breakfast
San Andreas, CA

 Mushrooms decrease in size when boiled.

ARTICHOKE DIP

Mix all ingredients in bowl. Cover, chill several hours or overnight. Serve with Pepperidge Farm English wafers.

Dunbar House Bed and Breakfast
Murphys, CA

1 14-ounce can artichoke hearts, drained and chopped

4 pieces bacon, crisply fried and crumbled

1 tablespoon minced onion

1 tablespoon fresh lemon juice

$\frac{1}{2}$ cup mayonnaise

dash of cayenne pepper

salt and pepper to taste

Worcestershire sauce to taste

SPICY YAM CAKES

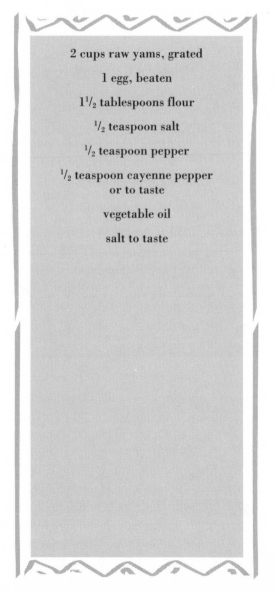

2 cups raw yams, grated

1 egg, beaten

1$\frac{1}{2}$ tablespoons flour

$\frac{1}{2}$ teaspoon salt

$\frac{1}{2}$ teaspoon pepper

$\frac{1}{2}$ teaspoon cayenne pepper
or to taste

vegetable oil

salt to taste

In a medium-size bowl, combine the first 6 ingredients and mix well. Set aside. Pour at least 1 inch of oil in a large skillet and heat until very hot. With 2 forks, about 1 tablespoon at a time, place the reserved yam mixture into the hot oil. Use forks to keep the cakes in a rounded shape. Cook until golden and crunchy. Drain on paper towels and sprinkle with salt. Serve hot.

Jan and Stephen Drammer and Jim Adams, Innkeepers
The Redbud Inn
Murphys, CA

MURPHYS HOTEL CRAB CAKES

Mix all ingredients, form into ¹/₂ inch thick, 3-ounce cakes. Cook in clarified butter at medium to medium-high until golden brown on both sides. Serve with lemon and tartar sauce.

Murphys Historic Hotel and Lodge
Murphys, CA

1 pound crab meat, well drained

¹/₄ cup mayonnaise

1 ounce lemon juice

2 ounces Worcestershire sauce

¹/₄ cup chopped chives

1¹/₂ ounces extra strong
Dijon mustard

1 egg

¹/₄ cup sourdough bread crumbs

lemon wedges and tartar sauce
for garnish

RICOTTA, PROSCIUTTO AND BASIL SPREAD

2 pounds ricotta cheese

$\frac{1}{2}$ cup olive oil

$\frac{1}{2}$ cup chopped garlic

$\frac{1}{2}$ pound thinly sliced prosciutto, cut into squares

1 cup chopped fresh basil

1 tablespoon freshly ground black pepper

Place ricotta cheese in large bowl and set aside. In a medium-size skillet, warm olive oil. Over medium heat, sauté garlic until golden brown, stirring frequently. Add prosciutto and heat until it begins to change color. Remove from heat.

Mix garlic and prosciutto with ricotta cheese, blending well. Add basil and pepper, and mix well. Place in serving bowl and serve with French bread, toast, crostini, or your favorite crackers. Try leftovers on pasta or in lasagna.

Dorrington Hotel and Restaurant
Dorrington, CA

ITALIAN FESTA

OAKLAND

Annual. Third Sunday in September.

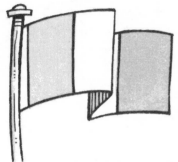

Ciao Italia! The annual Italian Festa brings Italy to Oakland. If it's true that food fuels the body, you'll get plenty of high octane at this fabulous festival.

Held at Jack London Square, this annual, one-day event features children's activities, Italian food, cultural exhibits, bocce ball demonstrations, Italian arts and crafts show, and an Italian entertainment, all in a fascinating waterfront setting.

You'll thoroughly enjoy the mouth-watering, authentic food booths featuring tempting selections prepared in the kitchens of East Bay's Italian Family Club. Food includes sausage sandwiches, polenta, pastas, pastries, and Italian ices and coffees. At night, the Square turns into an elegant Italian courtyard for live entertainment and dancing.

During the entire festival, bocce ball players perform and teach this traditional Italian game. Go ahead and try it. You'll discover that bocce is both challenging and exciting as you join or watch enthusiastic players pursue this competitive bowling game. It's still widely played in America by people of Italian descent.

Oakland is situated across the bay from San Francisco. A city of nearly 380,000 people, it's jam-packed with attractions, performing arts, affordable lodging, and taste-tempting restaurants.

To reach Jack London Square, take the Broadway exit off Interstate 880 and follow the signs to Embarcadero and Jack London Square.

LINGUINI PESCATORE

Sauce

$^1/_4$ cup olive oil

$^1/_2$ medium onion, chopped

2 cloves garlic, finely chopped

2 sprigs parsley, finely chopped

10 ounces crab meat

10 ounces shrimp meat

10 ounces clams or
2 dozen fresh clams

1 cup white wine

4 cups tomato sauce

salt and pepper to taste

$^3/_4$ cup sweet butter

1 pound linguini pasta

Heat olive oil and sauté onion until lightly brown. Add garlic and parsley and sauté. Add fish. When mixture is thoroughly heated, add white wine. After wine has evaporated, add tomato sauce. Salt and pepper to taste. Cook slowly for 15 minutes. Meanwhile, boil salted water for pasta. Cook al dente and drain. Add butter to sauce, pour over pasta to serve. Garnish with parsley.

Italian Festa
Oakland, CA

FIG & SUN-DRIED TOMATO PIZZA

Heat oil in large skillet; add onion, garlic, figs, and tomatoes. Cook until onions are tender. Stir in vinegar and basil. Sprinkle cheese evenly over pizza crust and top with fig mixture. Bake in preheated 425° oven until crust is browned, about 10 to 15 minutes. Cut into wedges to serve.

Carol Hughes
The California Fig Advisory Board
Fresno, CA

2 tablespoons olive oil

1 medium sweet or red onion, sliced

2 to 4 cloves garlic, minced

1 cup sliced California figs, stems removed

$1/4$ cup chopped sun-dried tomatoes

2 tablespoons balsamic vinegar

$1/4$ cup chopped fresh basil, oregano or Italian parsley

1 cup shredded part-skim mozzarella, provolone, or Monterey Jack cheese

1 12- to 14-inch prepared pizza crust or pizza bread base

GNOCCHI DI PATATE

Potato Dumplings

3 pounds potatoes, boiled
and mashed

3 cups all-purpose flour

$\frac{1}{2}$ cup butter

2 eggs, slightly beaten

salt to taste

In large bowl, combine mashed potatoes and flour and mix well, using hands. Crumble the butter into the flour and potato mixture, add eggs, and salt to taste; mix gently. Turn the potato dough onto a floured board and knead gently. Cut off small pieces of dough, gently shape into roll, about bread stick size, about 1 inch thick. Cut roll into inch-long pieces. Using 3 fingers or tongs of fork, shape each piece into a crescent. Continue until all dough is used. After shaping gnocchi, set aside on a floured surface, in single layers so they will not stick together.

To cook, drop dumplings into gently boiling salted water. Stir gently with wooden spoon for about 5 minutes. Dumplings will rise to top when cooked. Like all homemade pasta, it will cook quickly. Drain and serve with favorite meat sauce, pesto sauce, or butter and cheese.

Italian Festa
Oakland, CA

TURKEY BREAST FILLETS ALA MARSALA

Dip pounded turkey breast fillets in slightly beaten egg. Roll in French bread crumbs. Heat olive oil and butter in large skillet. Brown turkey fillets on both sides until golden, remove from skillet, keep warm. Add Marsala wine to skillet, bring to rolling boil, add mushrooms, salt, and pepper. Simmer a few minutes. Pour over fillets and serve immediately.

Irma DeLucci
Italian Festa
Oakland, CA

1 pound turkey breast fillets

1 egg

French bread crumbs

2 tablespoons olive oil

1 teaspoon butter

1 cup Marsala wine

1 cup mushrooms, thinly sliced

salt and pepper to taste

LAMBTOWN, U.S.A. FESTIVAL
DIXON
Annual. First weekend in August.

With each passing year, the annual Dixon Lambtown, U.S.A. Festival gets bigger and better. The festival is two days of seemingly never-ending fun, food, and entertainment.

Each year, more than 10,000 visitors take part in this celebration of Dixon's sheep and wool industry. Scheduled events include a roller blading event called Fun Roll, a fun run, livestock exhibits, and more. Backyard chefs show off their very best lamb recipes at the popular Lambtown Cook-Off Contest. From kabobs to fajitas, lamb is served in traditional and nontraditional food stops along "Lamb Lover's Lane."

The Mutton Bustin' Contest has enthusiastic youngsters between the ages of four and six competing to see who can ride a sheep for the longest time. Adults compete in the shearing championship, and monetary prizes are given to the contestant who shears the fastest.

Many of the more than sixty festival craft booths feature handcrafted lamb-theme items for sale. Even sheep dogs get their chance to compete during the Sheep Dog Trials where the dogs try to corral anything that moves.

No doubt you'll want to pick up a copy of the official *Dixon Lambtown, U.S.A. Festival Cookbook.* It's filled with some of the best lamb recipes you've ever tasted.

The following are all award-winning recipes from the Lambtown Cook-off Contest.

UNCLE ERNIE'S STUFFED LEG OF LAMB

Split boned leg lengthwise and pound until uniform in thickness. Combine first 7 ingredients of marinade, rub on both sides of meat. Cover and refrigerate for 12 hours in the marinade. Then add red wine and marinate an additional 12 hours.

Sauté spinach in olive oil, add mushrooms and chopped garlic cloves. Cook until tender. Set aside. In large bowl, soak bread crumbs in water until moist. Add spinach mixture.

Drain marinade from lamb and reserve for basting. Lay meat flat on aluminum foil. Lay prosciutto slices on lamb, spread stuffing mix on top. Roll up jelly roll-style and tie with string. Barbecue for approximately 1$1/2$ hours.

Uncle Ernie Nunes
Dixon, CA

3 to 5 pounds boned leg of lamb

10 to 15 slices prosciutto, sliced thin

Marinade
$1/4$ cup olive oil

2 tablespoons chopped garlic

2 tablespoons seasoned salt

3 tablespoons Italian seasoning

2 tablespoons parsley

3 tablespoons grated Parmesan cheese

1 onion, chopped fine

1 quart red wine

Stuffing
$1/4$ cup olive oil

1 large bag fresh spinach, chopped

1 pound large mushrooms, chopped

2 cloves garlic, chopped

1 bag bread crumbs

BIRRIA DE BORREGO

Mexican Lamb Stew

8 to 10 pounds lamb, with bones (shank or ribs)

Marinade

6 ounces dried pasilla chili pods

6 ounces dried New Mexico chili pods

6 whole, dried Japanese chilies, or substitute chili de arbol

2 teaspoons black peppercorns

10 cloves garlic, peeled

70 ounces canned whole tomatoes, undrained

2 teaspoons dried oregano

3 bay leaves

2 tablespoons sherry or white wine

3 teaspoons salt, or to taste

Garnish

chopped onions

fresh squeezed lemon juice

Boil pasilla and New Mexico chili pods (available in Mexican spice section of most supermarkets) until soft, in just enough water to cover. Remove stems and crush chili pods, blending with left-over hot water. Purée Japanese chilies, peppercorns, garlic, and canned tomatoes. Combine in deep bowl with oregano, bay leaves, sherry, and salt, mixing well.

Add additional chilies or spices to taste. Place lamb in roasting pan and top with $1/3$ of the marinade; cover pan tightly with heavy-duty aluminum foil. Bake at 350° for $2^1/_2$ to 3 hours, or until meat separates easily from the bone. Serve lamb in its own sauce, topped with chopped onions and lemon juice. Best eaten with fresh corn tortillas, rice, and beans. Makes enough marinade for 20 to 25 pounds of lamb.

Harry Barraza and Frank Leal
Dixon, CA

MID-SUMMER SCANDINAVIAN FESTIVAL

FERNDALE

Annual. Fourth weekend in June.

26

What could be better than free music, good food, and great times? That's what the Mid-Summer Scandinavian Festival is all about.

Don't waste a wonderful summer. Forget the chores, pack up the kids, and head out for a very special Scandinavian weekend. This is a festival where food is perfectly complemented by the natural and architectural setting. Here's your chance to celebrate the summer solstice with traditional Scandinavian music, authentic foods, dances, a flag ceremony, and a Grand March of costumes during this outstanding event. Æbleskiver is served hot from the pan, plus numerous booths provide Scandinavian food and arts and crafts.

Costumed tiny tots, young people, and adults get rave reviews as they perform traditional Scandinavian dances. On Sunday, the Grand March of colorful costumes is a highlight of the event and shouldn't be missed. Bring your camera, because you'll want to record the memories.

The minute you drive over the bridge into the Victorian village of Ferndale, you'll think you've stepped back a hundred years. Interestingly, the entire village has such historic importance it's been designated State Historical Landmark Number 883.

SPRUT COOKIES

1 cup butter

1 cup sugar

2 egg yolks and 1 whole egg
or 3 egg yolks

1 teaspoon vanilla

2½ cups flour

½ teaspoon baking powder

Cream butter and sugar. Add egg yolks and vanilla, then add flour and baking powder. Chill in refrigerator about 15 minutes. Put through cookie press, forming into figure "S" or round circles. Bake in 375° oven for about 8 minutes.

Eria Chance
Ferndale, CA

SWEDISH RYE BREAD

Pour the milk over the salt, molasses, and butter. Add the water. When cooled to lukewarm, add the yeast and white flour, and beat until smooth. Stir in the caraway seed. Gradually add the rye flour and mix to make a medium-stiff dough (it will be sticky). Turn it out on a floured board and knead until smooth (about 10 minutes).

Place in a buttered bowl, cover, and let rise until doubled (about 2 hours). Punch down and let rise again. Turn out and shape into 2 oblong loaves. Place on buttered cookie sheets that have been sprinkled with cornmeal. Let rise until doubled. Bake in a 375° oven for 30 to 40 minutes.

Marjorie Sieber
Ferndale, CA

1 cup scalded milk

$2\frac{1}{2}$ teaspoons salt

2 tablespoons molasses

2 tablespoons butter

1 cup water

1 cake yeast

$3\frac{1}{2}$ cups sifted white flour

1 tablespoon caraway seed

2 cups rye flour

cornmeal

DANISH MEATBALLS

$1^1/_2$ pounds ground beef

4 slices bread

$^1/_2$ pound ground pork

2 eggs

1 medium onion, chopped fine

1 teaspoon ground allspice

$^1/_4$ teaspoon ground cloves

touch of ginger

$^1/_4$ to $^1/_2$ cup warm water.

salt to taste

Put meats and bread through a meat grinder. Add eggs, onion, allspice, cloves, ginger, water, and salt. Mix well and roll into balls. Fry gently, rolling meatballs to retain shape until cooked thoroughly.

Helene Miller
Ferndale, CA

DANISH CUCUMBER SALAD

Agurkesalat

Peel and slice cucumbers paper thin. Sprinkle with salt and let stand 30 minutes. Squeeze cucumbers in your hand so all juice goes away. Place dried cucumbers in a glass jar. Mix vinegar with water, sugar, salt, and pepper. Heat to dissolve sugar, then pour over cucumbers. Let stand 3 to 4 hours to absorb flavors.

Agnes Andersen
Ferndale, CA

3 cucumbers

salt

1 cup vinegar

$1/2$ cup water

$1/2$ cup sugar

salt and pepper to taste

MOUNTAIN HARVEST FESTIVAL/ A TASTE OF QUINCY

QUINCY

Annual. Second Saturday in October.

27

In an area of rugged canyons, crystal clear lakes, grassy meadows, trout-filled streams, and fresh pine forests, residents, local restaurants, and helpful businesses combine efforts in celebration. They invite you to join them during their family-oriented event held on the courthouse lawn in the small community of Quincy.

It's a day filled with fun and surprises. The schedule includes a wide variety of tempting tastes, live entertainment, and action-packed activities. The Central Plumas Recreation District's Pumpkin Patch features pumpkins for sale. You get the opportunity to pick the perfect pumpkins for Halloween decorating and pumpkin pie baking.

You don't want to miss the creative and imaginative scarecrows displayed around town by many of the local merchants. They certainly add the right touch during the Children's Costume Parade. It's fun to watch as tiny ghosts, goblins, pirates, and clowns make their whimsical way down the parade's route.

Go ahead and take along your favorite pumpkin-based culinary delight. You can enter the Harvest Baking Contest, or help judge the contest with a $1 donation.

During A Taste of Quincy, you'll have your chance to sample appetizer-sized portions of cuisine prepared by several of the participating local restaurants. Pick up a ticket at the information booth for a fee. It's your invitation to tremendous tasting opportunities.

Hang around and enjoy the awards ceremony as the excitement builds and prizes are given honoring winners in the Costume Parade, Carved Pumpkin Contest, Harvest Baking Contest, and Scarecrow Contest.

GRILLED HERB-ENCRUSTED CHICKEN

Chop and combine herbs. Coat chicken with olive oil and roll in the chopped herbs. Grill on barbecue until done. Slice the chicken in julienne strips. In a bowl, combine olive oil and balsamic vinegar. Add mustard until mixture is smooth. Use as a dip or pour over chicken.

Moon Restaurant
Quincy, CA

 This recipe makes 96 appetizer-sized servings.

Herb Coating
(use fresh, coarsely chopped herbs)

2 bunches basil

2 bunches cilantro

1 bunch thyme

1 bunch oregano

1 bunch parsley

12 8-ounce chicken breasts

$1/2$ cup extra virgin olive oil

Sauce

1 cup extra virgin olive oil

$1/2$ cup balsamic vinegar

$1/2$ cup Dijon mustard

VEGITATERS

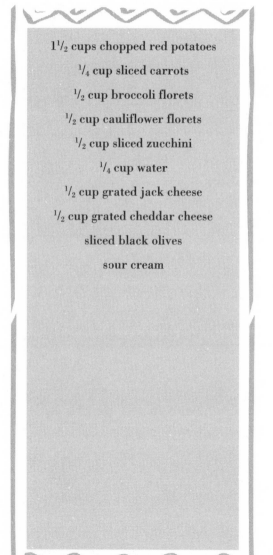

1½ cups chopped red potatoes

¼ cup sliced carrots

½ cup broccoli florets

½ cup cauliflower florets

½ cup sliced zucchini

¼ cup water

½ cup grated jack cheese

½ cup grated cheddar cheese

sliced black olives

sour cream

Fry potatoes on a grill until brown; transfer to skillet. Spread vegetables over hot grilled potatoes, add water, cover and steam until vegetables are al dente. Add cheeses and cover until cheese is melted. Serve with olives and sour cream.

Morning Thunder Cafe
Quincy, CA

PARMESAN-GLAZED HALIBUT FILLETS

Lightly pepper fillets. Combine all other ingredients. Spread even layer on fillets, bake in hot oven 15 to 20 minutes, depending on thickness of fish.

Ten-Two Dinner House
Quincy, CA

6 fresh halibut fillets

pepper to taste

$1/4$ cup lemon juice

2 cups grated Parmesan cheese

1 cup minced onion

$1/2$ cup mayonnaise

$1/2$ teaspoon salt

$1/8$ teaspoon Tabasco sauce

MUSHROOM MARDI GRAS

MORGAN HILL

Annual. Memorial Day weekend.

It's a family affair when Morgan Hill puts its best foods forward. Visitors flock from throughout the Bay Area and beyond to attend Mushroom Mardi Gras. You'll discover mushrooms in every size, shape, and variety. They'll be prepared in every imaginable way during this festival dedicated to the popular fungi. It is estimated that during the weekend more than a ton of mushrooms are used.

If you love mushrooms, you'll first want to head to Bon Appétit Square. Once there, you'll discover grilled mushroom kabobs, deep-fried mushrooms, mushroom pasta salad, and grilled portobello mushroom sandwiches. Other delicacies include stuffed and sautéed mushrooms, mushroom garlic bread, mushroom gelato, and marinated mushrooms. Even non-mushroom enthusiasts will find plenty to savor and taste.

In addition to food and plenty of live entertainment, the event features mushroom quizzes, all things from clothing to paintings for sale, a run for the mushrooms, and mushroom demonstration booths. You'll even learn about the various stages mushrooms go through as they grow to maturity.

Munchkinland is strictly for small fries. It includes a petting zoo, a jump house, and carnival games, and three times a day there's a parade led by musicians and jugglers.

All recipes in this section are from the Mushroom Mardi Gras.

MUSHROOM GARDEN BAKED POTATOES

Heat oil in 8x10-inch skillet. Add mushrooms, bell pepper, and garlic. Cook until mushrooms are lightly brown. Add water and lemon juice. Reduce heat to low and cook 3 minutes. Season with salt and pepper. Split and fluff potatoes and top with mushroom mixture.

2 tablespoons olive oil

8 ounces fresh mushrooms, sliced

1 small red bell pepper, seeded, cut into 1-inch squares

1 large clove garlic, minced

2 tablespoons water

$1^1/_2$ tablespoons lemon juice

salt and pepper to taste

2 baked potatoes, 6 ounces each

COLD & SPICY MUSHROOM NOODLES

8 ounces fine or medium egg noodles

8 ounces asparagus, fresh, sliced diagonally

1 tablespoon vegetable oil

8 ounces fresh mushrooms, sliced

Cold and Spicy Sauce

3 tablespoons vegetable oil

2 tablespoons peanut butter

2 tablespoons soy sauce

2 tablespoons water

1 teaspoon sugar

$1/4$ to $1/2$ teaspoon chili flakes

Garnish

3 tablespoons green onions, sliced thin

In 2- or 3-quart saucepan, cook noodles in boiling water until done, about 6 to 8 minutes. Drain, cover with cold water until ready to use. Sauté asparagus in oil until just tender, add mushrooms. Toss and chill.

In electric blender, combine all sauce ingredients and blend for one minute. In large bowl, combine noodles, asparagus, and sauce. Arrange on a platter and garnish with green onions.

You may substitue seasonal vegetables for the asparagus. Try snow peas, green beans, or broccoli.

TUXEDO MUSHROOM BURGERS

In skillet, sauté mushrooms in butter with the garlic, 1 teaspoon of the oregano, and salt and pepper, until tender. Remove from heat. Stir in Parmesan cheese. Keep mixture warm. Season beef with remaining teaspoon of oregano, and salt and pepper. Form into 4 to 6 equal balls. Make a large depression in each, fill cavities with half of the sautéed mushrooms, dividing equally. Bring beef up around mushrooms to enclose, pressing gently to form into patties. Broil or grill until cooked through. Top with remaining sautéed mushrooms. Serve with sour cream or mustard.

8 ounces fresh mushrooms, sliced

butter or margarine

2 cloves garlic, pressed

2 teaspoons leaf oregano

salt and pepper to taste

$1/4$ cup Parmesan cheese

2 pounds ground beef

MUSTARD FESTIVAL

NAPA VALLEY
Annual. February and March.

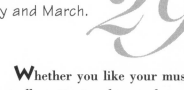

Whether you like your mustard mellow, sweet and tangy, hot and spicy, or plain yellow, you'll discover there are more types of mustard than you ever imagined. Domestic and international mustards will satisfy and delight the most discerning palate.

The two-month long Mustard Festival is Napa Valley's celebration of world-class wine, regional cuisine, fine art, and the annual bounty of wild mustard. The Valley's hillsides, valleys, and vineyards come alive with golden flowering mustard from about mid-January through March each year. When they do, Napa Valley welcomes the season with a variety of special events.

Specific events change each year, but no matter when you attend, you'll discover two months filled with outstanding food, wine, art, and mustard celebrations. There are special winemaker dinners, mustard and gourmet food tastings, balloon ascensions, running marathons, workshops, and live entertainment at venue locations scattered throughout the Valley.

Legend has it that the present-day wild mustard plants are descendants of the seeds scattered by Franciscan Padre Serra when he explored Napa Valley in the early 1800s. You'll agree that it's a brilliant and inspiring legacy.

WHOLE-GRAIN MUSTARD POTATO SALAD

Steam potatoes until tender. Chill immediately with ice. When cool, quarter potatoes, leaving skin intact. In a large sauté pan, heat olive oil, sauté onion until tender. Add potatoes, salt, and pepper; toss gently. Add mustard, sherry vinegar, and parsley. Toss gently. Adjust seasoning to taste. Serve while still warm.

Executive Chef David Hall
Auberge du Soleil
Rutherford, CA

 Delicious served with smoked duck sausage.

2 pounds red bliss potatoes

2 ounces olive oil

salt and pepper to taste

1 large red onion, julienned

1 ounce whole-grain mustard

2 ounces sherry vinegar

2 tablespoons chopped parsley

WARM PEACH-MUSTARD COMPOTE

1 small onion, diced

3 whole ripe peaches, peeled, diced

1 tablespoon maple syrup

4 ounces mild brown mustard

2 tablespoons chopped parsley

cracked black pepper to taste

Sauté onion in butter over medium heat until tender and translucent, approximately 5 minutes. Remove from heat. Add diced peaches and maple syrup. Toss gently. Transfer mixture into a medium bowl. Fold in mustard, parsley, and pepper. Refrigerate at least 4 hours. Heat and serve.

Executive Chef David Hall
Auberge du Soleil
Rutherford, CA

 Serve warm with baked ham or grilled meats and sausages.

BROILED PACIFIC SALMON WITH TAPENADE OF CALAMATA OLIVE, SUN-DRIED TOMATO, AND LEEK, SERVED WITH CHEF'S COMPOUND BUTTER

For tapenade, finely dice olives, sun-dried tomatoes, and leeks. Keep separate until 1 hour before serving, then combine ingredients with sherry vinegar and olive oil. Set aside.

Sauté garlic, shallot, red onion, thyme. Flame with vermouth. Burn off alcohol. Set aside in a mixer. Soften butter. Add sautéed ingredients, Worcestershire sauce, and Tabasco. Pipe butter stars onto cookie sheet, refrigerate.

Broil salmon to desired doneness. Garnish with 2 teaspoons of tapenade and top fish with star of compound butter.

Chef Patrick Finney
Napa Valley Wine Train
Napa, CA

 The Napa Valley Wine Train offers a 3-hour, nonstop, round trip, gourmet dining and sightseeing tour on 1900s Pullman cars.

¼ cup Calamata olives

¼ cup sun-dried tomatoes

¼ cup fresh leeks

1 ounce sherry vinegar

3 tablespoons olive oil

Chef's Compound Butter

1 tablespoon garlic

1 shallot

¼ cup red onion

2 tablespoons fresh thyme

1 cup sweet vermouth

1 pound unsalted butter

2 tablespoons Worcestershire sauce

splash of Tabasco

4 6-ounce pieces of fresh salmon

MIXED GRILL OF SEAFOOD

Trio of homemade mustards

1 pound large sea scallops
1 pound fresh tuna
1 pound large shrimp
olive oil
salt and pepper to taste

Honey Dijon Mustard
1 ounce honey
4 ounces white wine
2 ounces Colmans dry mustard
1 egg, beaten

Whole Grain Apricot Mustard
2 ounces whole mustard seed
4 ounces apricot jam
(preferably whole fruit)
4 ounces water

Ginger Wasabi Mustard
$1/2$ ounce dry mustard powder
1 ounce wasabi powder
2 ounces rice wine vinegar
1 ounce chopped pickled ginger

Brush all seafood with olive oil, salt and pepper. Over a hot grill, cook all seafood to desired doneness. Serve on a plate with accompanying mustards and any rice or vegetable desired.

Honey Dijon Mustard: Bring honey and wine to a boil in a small saucepan. Whip in dry mustard, simmer for 5 minutes. Whip in egg, cool, and refrigerate overnight.

Whole-Grain Apricot Mustard: Combine all ingredients in a small saucepan. Simmer gently for 15 minutes. Cool and refrigerate overnight.

Ginger Wasabi Mustard: In a small saucepan, bring rice vinegar to a boil, fold in mustard and wasabi. Remove from heat, cool to room temperature, fold in pickled ginger. Refrigerate overnight.

Auberge du Soleil
Rutherford, CA

SAUTÉED PORK MEDALLIONS WITH WHOLE-GRAIN MUSTARD AND SPICY GRAPES

Spicy Grapes: Mix all ingredients, except grapes, in a large saucepan. Bring to a boil, mixing thoroughly. Add grapes and let cool for at least 2 hours to develop flavor.

Pound out pork medallions to about $1/4$ inch thick, season with salt and pepper and lightly dredge in flour. Sauté in a hot pan with the olive oil approximately 1 minute per side or until nicely browned all over. Set aside. Add shallots to pan that is still hot and cook briefly so they do not brown. Add vermouth and reduce to a glaze. Add mustards, chicken stock, and one cup spicy grapes (with some of their juices). Reduce by $1/3$ and finish by adding the butter and swirling it in the pan until incorporated into the sauce. Add pork to pan, reheat, and serve.

Executive Chef Bob Hurley
Napa Valley Grille
Yountville, CA

2 pork tenderloins, cleaned and cut into $1^1/_2$-inch slices

salt and pepper to taste

flour

2 tablespoons olive oil

4 tablespoons chopped shallots

2 ounces dry vermouth

2 tablespoons whole-grain mustard

1 tablespoon Dijon mustard

5 ounces chicken stock (rich)

1 ounce butter

Spicy Grapes

$1^1/_2$ cups sugar

$1^1/_2$ cups cider vinegar

2 tablespoons crushed coriander seeds

1 tablespoon crushed cumin seeds

1 tablespoon fresh orange zest

1 tablespoon ground cinnamon

7 whole cloves

1 teaspoon salt

8 slices fresh, peeled ginger

3 jalapeño peppers with seeds, sliced thin

3 cups red and green seedless grapes

ONION FESTIVAL

VACAVILLE

Annual. September date varies.

For more than fifty years Vacaville has been identified by the odor of onions being processed. Some say that anyone traveling between Sacramento and San Francisco knows when they're in Vacaville from the onion aroma.

The Vacaville Onion Festival celebrates the onion during two days of nonstop action. Activities dedicated to the onion include plenty of food concessions, arts and crafts, demonstration kitchens, entertainment, and (hold your nose!) an onion eating contest.

You'll be amazed at how versatile the onion can be. Those of us who love cooking with onions always discover new recipes and uses during the festival. You may want to pick up a copy of *The Onion Ring Cookbook,* a compilation of information and recipes. According to the cookbook's introduction, "The time has come that one of the most misunderstood vegetables the world has ever known be given the recognition it deserves."

It was 1841 when the King of Spain granted more than eighty thousand acres to Manuel Vaca and Felip Pena. Fifty-one years later the area was incorporated as a city. When you check your California map, you'll find Vacaville located in Solano County, on Interstate 80, about 30 miles southwest of Sacramento, the state capital.

PEARL ONIONS IN RASPBERRY WINE VINEGAR SAUCE

In large skillet, heat butter and oil. Add garlic salt, thyme, rosemary, basil, paprika, and onion powder. Add onions, sauté gently until golden brown, being careful not to burn. Remove onions with slotted spoon. Keep warm. Deglaze skillet with raspberry wine vinegar. Add chicken stock. Slowly blend in whipping cream. Add red wine. Return pearl onions to sauce. Simmer for 30 minutes. Add additional raspberry wine vinegar, garlic salt, and ground pepper to taste.

Joan Costas Nicholes
Onion Festival Cook-off Winner

 Serve over wild rice or as hors d'oeuvres.

3 tablespoons butter

2 tablespoons extra virgin olive oil

1 teaspoon garlic salt

$^1/_2$ teaspoon thyme

$^1/_2$ teaspoon rosemary

$^1/_4$ teaspoon basil

$^1/_2$ teaspoon paprika

1 teaspoon onion powder

3 cups pearl onions

$^3/_4$ cup raspberry wine vinegar

1 cup chicken stock

2 cups whipping cream

$^1/_2$ cup red wine

raspberry wine vinegar, to taste

garlic salt and ground pepper to taste

VORACIOUS VACAVILLE BURGERS

1 cup purple onions

1 cup white onions

$1/2$ cup yellow onions

1 bunch green onions
(reserve tops for garnish)

1 large clove garlic

3 tablespoons butter

pinch of salt

pinch of cayenne pepper

$1/2$ cup fresh basil, chopped

$1/2$ cup (total) yellow, red and
green peppers

$2/3$ cup fresh Parmesan cheese,
grated

3 cups fresh small sourdough
bread pieces

2 cups canned French-fried
onion rings

1 egg

1 medium bag potato chips, crushed

3 tablespoons sunflower oil

olive oil and shredded lettuce
(for garnish)

fresh sourdough bread slices

Dice and sauté all the "sassy onions" and garlic in butter. Add salt, cayenne, basil, and half of the peppers. Set aside half of the peppers and green onion tops for garnish. Remove from heat and place in a bowl. Add cheese, bread, onion rings, and eggs. Gently fold and make into patties.

Roll in crushed potato chips and fry in oil at medium heat until golden brown. Drain patties on paper towel for a second. Serve as soon as possible on a slice of sourdough bread. Garnish with lettuce, remaining peppers, green onion tops, and olive oil.

Alannah Ashlie-Vinke
1st Place Cook-off Winner

BAKED STUFFED ONION ENCHILADAS

Preheat oven to 350°. Grease a 9x13-inch pan with butter. Mix together sour cream, 1 can of the chilies, and the mushroom soup. Set mixture aside. Cut the four large onions in half. Hollow out the inside of each onion so that it resembles a bowl, leaving approximately $1/2$ to 1 inch of onion all around. Set aside. Sauté garlic and chopped onions in 1 tablespoon of butter on low heat until soft. Add mushrooms, broth, meat, and enchilada mix. Simmer, stirring constantly for 5 minutes.

Spread a small amount of the sour cream sauce over the bottom of the pan. Fill the onion bowls almost to the top with meat mixture. Arrange the bowls side by side in the pan. Pour remaining sauce equally over each bowl. Cover loosely with foil and bake for 30 minutes. Remove foil. Top each bowl with cheddar cheese, remaining can of green chilies, and chopped red pepper. Bake an extra 3 to 5 minutes, until cheese is melted.

Linda Dougherty
Vacaville, CA

12 ounces sour cream

2 4-ounce cans chopped green chilies

1 can cream of mushroom soup

4 large onions

1 clove garlic, minced

$1/2$ cup chopped onion

1 tablespoon butter or margarine

1 8-ounce can sliced mushrooms, undrained

1 cup canned chicken broth (or beef broth, if using ground beef)

4 cups chopped cooked chicken (or cooked ground beef)

1 1.62-ounce envelope enchilada sauce mix

2 cups shredded cheddar cheese

$1/2$ cup chopped red pepper

OYSTER FESTIVAL
ARCATA
Annual. June weekend.

Seventeenth-century writer John Pomfret once wrote, "He was a bold man that first ate an oyster." Today, some folks still shudder at the thought of downing one of the tasty morsels.

Nearly ninety percent of the oysters produced in California are harvested in Arcata, and the annual Arcata Bay Oyster Festival pays homage to this sometimes maligned small sea animal.

During the event, thirty local restaurants serve their finest oyster delicacies. This is the time to learn about the economy of sea harvests, watch a zany oyster shucking and calling contest, view large ice sculptures, listen to music, and eat oysters served baked, fried, and poached. Musical entertainment includes jazz and calypso rhythms, and Fred Oystaire (get the pun?) fills the event site with merriment and outlandish frivolity.

Whether you like plump and juicy oysters chilled, on the half shell, or served with cocktail sauce, the entire family will have a great time eating. You'll also want to take time to visit several aquatic shows and learn about boats, rafts, and kayaks. Take along the wee ones. They can get up close and cozy with small animals in the petting zoo and be entertained by magicians and puppeteers. Hey, you may even get lucky and have your photograph taken with Madam Mollusk, the annual Oyster Queen.

GRILLED OYSTERS AND CLAMS WITH SPICY CAJUN SAUCE

Place oysters and clams on ungreased grill 4 to 5 inches over hot coals. Cover with lid or aluminum foil. Cook until oysters and clams begin to open, 5 to 10 minutes, depending on size. Place on a platter.

Spicy Cajun Sauce: Sauté bacon in saucepan until browned. Drain off and discard fat. Add onion and sauté until tender. Stir in chili powder, pepper, and cumin, sauté 1 minute. Add remaining ingredients and cook over low heat, stirring occasionally, for 30 minutes or until sauce is somewhat thickened.

Open and discard top shells. Spoon a little Spicy Cajun Sauce onto each. Return to the grill and cook, covered, about 2 minutes longer or until sauce bubbles. Serve hot.

The National Fisheries Institute
Arlington, VA

---

2 dozen oysters (about $1^1/_2$ ounces each) in the shell, scrubbed

2 dozen clams (about 1 ounce each) in the shell, scrubbed

Spicy Cajun Sauce

2 strips of bacon, finely chopped

$^1/_3$ cup onion, finely chopped

$^3/_4$ teaspoon chili powder

$^1/_4$ teaspoon black pepper

$^1/_4$ teaspoon ground cumin

1 cup bottled chili sauce

$^2/_3$ cup orange juice

$^1/_4$ cup honey

3 tablespoons cider vinegar

2 large cloves garlic, minced

OYSTERS ROCKEFELLER PIZZA

1 clove garlic, minced

1 teaspoon olive oil

4 cups torn fresh spinach, lightly packed

2 tablespoons chopped green onion

$1/2$ cup tomato sauce

2 drops hot sauce

1 $9^1/_2$-ounce focaccia bread

1 $3^3/_4$-ounce can smoked oysters, drained and coarsely chopped

1 tablespoon bacon bits (optional)

4 ounces each mozzarella and provolone cheeses

Sauté garlic in oil for 1 minute, add spinach and onion, cook until spinach is wilted. Stir in tomato sauce and hot sauce. Spread spinach mixture on focaccia bread. Top with oysters, bacon, and cheeses. Place on baking sheet, bake at 350° for 6 to 10 minutes, or until cheese is melted and heated through.

National Fisheries Institute
Arlington, VA

PUMPKIN ORANGE OYSTER BISQUE

In a 4-quart pot, place broth and pumpkin. Stir until blended, bring to a boil, and reduce the heat to low. Cover and simmer 10 minutes. Place 1 cup of the soup and the cream cheese in a blender and whirl until smooth. Return to the soup pot, add the orange juice and oysters with liquor. Simmer 3 minutes. Add the rest of the ingredients and heat until hot.

Roxanne E. Chan
Albany, CA

 This award-winning recipe is included in the official *National Oyster Cook-Off* cookbook.

1 quart chicken broth

1 16-ounce can solid-packed pumpkin

1 3-ounce package cream cheese, cubed

2 cups orange juice

$1\frac{1}{2}$ pints fresh, shucked Maryland oysters with liquor

$\frac{1}{2}$ cup minced shallots

2 green onions, minced

$\frac{1}{2}$ chopped parsley

1 tablespoon grated orange peel

$\frac{1}{2}$ teaspoon coarsely ground black pepper

OYSTERS WITH SPINACH PESTO

3 garlic cloves, chopped

$1/3$ cup extra virgin olive oil

$1^1/_2$ cups firmly packed fresh spinach, stems removed

$1/2$ cup firmly packed parsley sprigs, stems removed (preferably Italian flat leaf)

$1/4$ cup walnut pieces

$1/2$ cup feta cheese

2 dozen Maryland oysters, shucked and on the half shell

Preheat oven to 500°. To prepare pesto, place the garlic and oil in a blender or food processor and blend until smooth. Add spinach, parsley, walnuts, and cheese. Cover and blend until smooth. Scrape sides with a rubber spatula as needed.

Spread $2^1/_2$ teaspoons of the pesto on top of each oyster. Place the oysters in 500° oven for 3 to 5 minutes. If preferred, place oysters on a grill until they are barely cooked and the topping is hot, about 5 to 7 minutes.

Barri Altimari
Rescue, CA

 This award-winning original appetizer is included in the official *National Oyster Cook-Off* cookbook.

PEAR FAIR

COURTLAND

Annual. Last Sunday in July.

The Pear Fair celebrates the Sacramento River Delta's famous Bartlett pear harvest. Held in Courtland, several small communities join together to honor this fabulous fruit.

One of the highpoints of the day is the delightful hometown parade. It features the Pear Fair Royalty Court, the Courtland Volunteer Fire Department, antique cars, twins contest entrants, local floats, and entertainers. Who wouldn't get a lump in the throat as banners and flags fly, small children smile, and old-timers give thanks for the harvest?

You'll want to join in when you see the delicious, down-home pear food: pear pies, pear fritters, pear parfaits, pear frappés, pear juice, pear sundaes, pear crepes, and fresh pears. Oh, yes, don't forget to begin your day at the pancake breakfast. How's that for indulging your palate? The arts and crafts section features approximately seventy-five craftspeople displaying their wares, and the Courtland Post Office offers a special Pear Fair stamp cancellation.

Contests abound. You may want to guess the number of pears in a bin, or join in pie-eating, pear-peeling, and pear-weighing contests. The competition is keen but the contestants have a great time trying to top one another's efforts.

The Pear Industry Historical Display includes orchard and picking equipment, lug boxes, sorting tables, fruit jars, early delta area photographs, and a label collection.

All recipes for this section were provided by the organizers of the Courtland Pear Fair.

PEAR COBBLER

1 29-ounce can pear halves.
Drain and reserve 1 cup syrup

$1/4$ cup flour

$1/2$ teaspoon grated lemon peel

$1/4$ teaspoon salt

dash of ginger

1 cup ginger ale

1 tablespoon butter

1 can Pillsbury Refrigerator Quick
Caramel Rolls with nuts

Cube pears, place in 2-quart casserole. In saucepan, combine flour, lemon peel, salt, ginger, ginger ale, reserved syrup, and sugar nut mixture from can of caramel rolls. Mix well. Cook over medium heat, stirring occasionally until thick. Stir in butter. Pour over pears. Separate caramel rolls, arrange on top of sauce. Bake at 400° for 25 to 30 minutes, until golden brown. Serve warm.

QUICK PEAR BREAD

Cream together shortening and sugars. Add egg, beat. Sift together flour, soda, allspice, cinnamon, and salt. Add to shortening mixture, stir in pears and nuts. Pour into a 9-inch greased loaf pan. Bake at 350° for 1 hour. Let stand until cool. Remove bread from pan. Sprinkle with powdered sugar for added taste.

$^1/_2$ cup shortening

$^1/_2$ cup brown sugar

$^1/_2$ cup sugar

1 egg

2 cups flour

1 teaspoon baking soda

$^1/_2$ teaspoon allspice

1 teaspoon cinnamon

$^1/_2$ teaspoon salt

2 cups chopped fresh pears

$^2/_3$ cup chopped nuts

powdered sugar (optional)

PEAR-RASPBERRY JAM

1 10-ounce box frozen raspberries

about 5 pears

$^1/_4$ cup lemon juice

1 tablespoon grated orange peel

6 cups sugar

$^1/_2$ bottle liquid pectin

Thaw raspberries and add pears to make 4 cups. Put in kettle with lemon juice, orange rind, and sugar. Bring to hard boil. Boil for one minute, stirring. Remove from heat and stir in pectin. Ladle into jars.

BAKED PEARS

Wipe, halve, and core pears. Put into deep dish, sprinkle with brown sugar or molasses. Dot with butter. Add small amount of water to prevent burning, cover, and bake 30 minutes at 350°. Serve with spice cake, or top with ice cream, orange sherbet, whipped cream, or sour cream.

Variations: Stuff centers with honey and almonds or butter and mincemeat, or sprinkle with ginger, lemon juice, or rum.

 Baked pears are delicious warm or cold.

 Drizzle a teaspoon of brandy over each baked pear before serving.

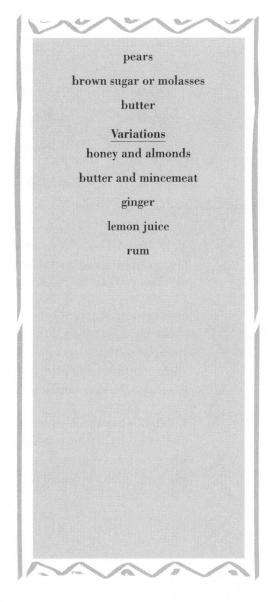

pears

brown sugar or molasses

butter

Variations

honey and almonds

butter and mincemeat

ginger

lemon juice

rum

PEAR FESTIVAL

KELSEYVILLE

Annual. Third Saturday in October.

33

There's more to this event than just a bushel of pears. For one day, all of Kelseyville, the "Bartlett Pear Capital of the World," becomes addicted to delicious and healthy pears. This downtown festival includes a highly regarded quilt show where you'll see some of California's finest old and new quilts on display and for sale.

The festival starts with a parade along Kelseyville's Main Street. Then, the festival begins. There's a pear-packing contest, a pear toss, pear activities, and pear displays from various pear-packing houses. Go ahead, see how fast you can say "pick a pack of perfect pears."

Festival organizers pride themselves in putting on a quality festival geared to the entire family. There's always a petting zoo of barnyard animals and pony rides for youngsters. Everyone enjoys the cool and easy music, food, live entertainment, and crafts. If you want a ride to all the action on Main Street, there's a horse-drawn wagon to take everyone around the event site.

Kelseyville is a small, country town located in California's north coast region, at Clear Lake. The lake is the state's largest natural freshwater lake. Consider taking several days to visit the lake region. Activities such as fishing, boating, water-skiing, camping, and sailing abound.

PEAR-PISTACHIO FRUIT CHEWS

Process dried fruits, pistachios, orange peel and juice in food processor until mixture is finely chopped and sticking together in a mass, about 1 minute. Divide mixture into 16 equal pieces and shape into blocks. Coat blocks with powdered sugar, shake off excess sugar.

Note: if you do not have a food processor, finely chop fruits and pistachios together on cutting board (the nuts keep the fruit from sticking to knife). Combine fruit-nut mixture with orange peel and juice, then shape and coat as above.

California Pistachio Commission
Fresno, CA

 To keep pistachios fresh, store in an airtight container and refrigerate.

$^1/_2$ cup dried pears

1 cup dried apples

$^3/_4$ cup golden raisins

$^1/_2$ cup natural California pistachios, chopped

2 teaspoons grated orange peel

2 teaspoons orange juice

3 tablespoons sifted powdered sugar

PEAR-PORK WILD RICE SALAD

1 6-ounce package white and
wild rice mix

8 cups mixed, torn salad greens

$^1/_2$ pound carrots, julienne or thinly
sliced strips

$^1/_2$ red onion, thinly sliced

$^1/_4$ pound pea pods, optional

10 ounces well-trimmed, cooked,
and chilled roast pork or chicken,
thinly sliced

4 fresh California Bartlett pears

low fat bottled Italian dressing

To prepare rice, cook as directed but omit butter, then refrigerate. Meanwhile, toss greens with carrots, onion slices, and pea pods. Line 4 individual salad plates with salad mixture. Scoop chilled rice into center. Top with chilled pork or chicken and sliced pears. Drizzle with dressing.

California Pear Advisory Board
Sacramento, CA

PEARS, PORT, AND STILTON CHEESE

On a serving platter, arrange pear slices and walnuts around the wedge of cheese. Serve with your favorite glass of port or red wine.

California Pear Advisory Board
Sacramento, CA

2 fresh California Bartlett pears, cored and thickly sliced

1 cup shelled, toasted walnut halves, optional

1 wedge aged English Stilton cheese or other blue-veined cheese

port or red wine

EXQUISITE PEAR & SPINACH SALAD

Blue Cheese Croutons

3 slices bread, cut into $\frac{1}{2}$-inch pieces (about 3 cups)

2 tablespoons butter

2 tablespoons Stilton blue cheese

Mustard Vinaigrette

2 tablespoons minced shallot (about 1 small shallot)

2 tablespoons rice wine vinegar

1 teaspoon fresh ground black pepper

salt to taste

1 tablespoon country-style Dijon mustard

2 tablespoons walnut oil

8 tablespoons olive oil

Salad

1 6-ounce package baby spinach or torn spinach leaves

2 fresh California Bartlett pears, sliced

$\frac{1}{2}$ cup walnuts, toasted

3 cups Stilton blue cheese croutons

$\frac{3}{4}$ cup whole-grain mustard vinaigrette

4 grilled boneless chicken breasts, sliced (optional)

1 tablespoon Stilton blue cheese

To prepare croutons, place cubed bread in bowl. Over medium heat, melt butter and blue cheese, stirring constantly. Pour cheese over cubed bread and toss thoroughly. Place bread on baking sheet. Bake at 350° until golden brown, about 10 to 15 minutes. Set aside to cool.

To prepare vinaigrette, combine shallot, vinegar, pepper, salt, and mustard in a small bowl; whisk in oils.

To prepare salad, toss spinach, pears, walnuts, and croutons in a large bowl. Add vinaigrette and toss. Line platter or 4 individual plates with salad. Top with sliced chicken. Crumble the blue cheese on top of each salad and serve.

Chef Jim LaPerriere
Enotria Cafe and Wine Bar
Sacramento, CA

 This recipe was created by Chef Jim LaPerriere exclusively for the California Pear Advisory Board.

PRUNE FESTIVAL

YUBA CITY
Annual. Weekend after Labor Day.

Go ahead and wear plum. Lots of folks do when they attend this celebration of all that's good about prunes. Held at the Yuba-Sutter Fairgrounds in Yuba City, it's the place to enjoy prunes in all shapes, sizes, activities, and food delicacies.

Six stages provide entertainment, including jazz, dixieland, Obon dancers, jugglers, and sounds that suit nearly every musical taste. Children have a fun and entertaining area designed just for them. There, they'll enjoy clowns, puppeteers, a petting zoo, and hands-on workshops. Both adults and children will relish the variety found in the Artisans' Village and additional sites that offer photography, farmers' market items, floral exhibits and displays, plus food and ice carving demonstrations.

Don't forget to step inside the Prune Pavilion. It's there you'll discover a variety of information you probably never knew about prunes. You'll also get a chance to taste prune pasta, prune yogurt, prune cake, and dozens of other prune-flavored foods.

California produces about seventy percent of the world's prune supply. With almost one-third of California's prune acreage in Yuba and Sutter counties, the area has a rightful claim to the title of Prune Capital of the World.

All recipes from this festival also appear in the *California Prune Festival Cookbook.*

FILLET OF PORK
WITH PRUNE SAUCE

3 pounds pork loin, cut in thin, wide strips

3 tablespoons olive oil

$3/4$ to 1 cup green onions, chopped

1 cup prunes, pitted, coarsely chopped

$3/4$ cup rice wine

$1/2$ cup prune juice

$1/4$ cup red wine vinegar

$1/4$ cup teriyaki sauce

$1/8$ cup cornstarch mixed with $1/4$ cup water

$1/8$ cup hot Chinese mustard

1 teaspoon granulated garlic

Brown pork in olive oil in heavy skillet over medium-high heat. Remove pork. Sauté green onions and prunes, add rice wine, prune juice, red wine vinegar, and teriyaki sauce. Cook until bubbly. Add cornstarch mixture and Chinese mustard. Continue cooking until thick.

Put a layer ($1/2$) of pork in bottom of a 9x12-inch casserole dish. Season meat with garlic. Pour $1/2$ of prune sauce over first layer of pork. Repeat with a second layer of pork. Pour remaining sauce over meat and cover. Bake for 1 hour and 15 minutes in a 350° oven. Let sit for 15 minutes.

Debbie O'Neal

 Serve this dish over long grain rice and garnish with chopped green onions.

PRUNE COUSCOUS

Melt butter over medium heat in a 2-quart saucepan. Add almonds and onions. Stir-fry almonds and onions for 2 to 3 minutes, until onions are slightly browned. Add prunes, broth, prune juice, and herbs. Bring mixture to a boil, cover, reduce heat, and simmer for 5 minutes. Remove lid and stir in couscous. Return to a boil and cook for 2 more minutes with the cover on. Turn off heat.

Fluff with a fork a couple of times before serving. Mound Prune Couscous on a serving platter and garnish with sliced, toasted almonds and minced green onions.

Frances Benthin

 An excellent side dish to serve with chicken, pork, or an Asian entrée.

2 tablespoons butter

$^{1}/_{2}$ cup sliced almonds

1 cup chopped onion

1 cup diced pitted prunes

1 cup chicken broth

$^{1}/_{2}$ cup prune juice

1 tablespoon mixed herbs

1 cup couscous

green onions and sliced almonds for garnish

BETTER'N MOM'S PRUNE CAKE

1½ cups unbleached white flour

1 cup whole-wheat flour

1 teaspoon baking soda

2 teaspoons baking powder

¼ teaspoon salt

1 teaspoon cinnamon

¼ teaspoon ground cloves

dash of freshly grated nutmeg

4 eggs at room temperature

¾ cup granulated sugar

¾ cup light brown sugar

¾ cup corn oil

¾ cup dark rum (1 cup of buttermilk, 1 tablespoon grated orange rind, and 1 teaspoon vanilla may be substituted for rum)

1¾ cups coarsely cut cooked dried prunes

¾ cup chopped walnuts

Glaze

1 tablespoon butter or margarine

1 cup sifted powdered sugar

2½ tablespoons dark rum (orange juice with 1 teaspoon grated orange rind may be substituted for rum)

2 tablespoons finely chopped walnuts

Combine flours, baking soda, baking powder, salt, cinnamon, cloves, and nutmeg, stir with fork to mix, and set aside. Beat eggs in large mixing bowl, add sugars, and beat thoroughly. With mixer running, add oil and beat until well blended. By hand, fold in dry ingredients in thirds, alternating with two additions of rum. Add prunes and nuts before the last addition of dry ingredients. Mix well. Turn into well-greased, 12-cup fluted tube pan. Bake at 350° for 50 minutes or until cake tests done. Cool upright in pan for 15 minutes, invert and remove from pan. Cool thoroughly.

While cake is cooling, prepare glaze. Melt butter or margarine, remove from heat, and stir in powdered sugar and rum. Drizzle glaze over cake and immediately sprinkle with chopped nuts.

Chris Schulz

PUMPKIN-FEST

HEALDSBURG

Annual. Saturday closest to Halloween.

Folks in Healdsburg are crazy about pumpkins. They celebrate each year by throwing a bright orange festival in the town's historic Healdsburg Plaza.

The fun begins in the morning as everyone takes part in the hilarious pumpkin-carving competition. You'll have a great time if you join others in some creative carving. The festival supplies everything needed except the artistic talent.

While the carving goes on, local cooks and chefs busily put the finishing touches on some of the best pumpkin delicacies you've ever tasted. The food is fabulous. There's no restriction on size or shape, but all recipes must contain pumpkin in the list of ingredients. If you feel like flexing your pecs, join the excitement of the pumpkin-carrying contest. The contest is a high point during the day's perfect pumpkin party. If you lose, don't fret. Most of the losing pumpkins end up being eaten—often as part of a delicious pie.

You'll find it tempting to fill up on pumpkin delicacies. But save room to visit one of Healdsburg's thirty restaurants, five coffeehouses, and six bakeries. When you feel the need for libations, there are more than fifty wineries surrounding the city, with two operating within a few blocks of the center of town.

After attending the Pumpkin-Fest, eating great food and sampling fine wine, you'll be heard repeating over and over, "Peter Piper picked plentiful pumpkins participating in a perfect pumpkin party."

MY NUTTY PUMPKIN PIE

1 unbaked pie crust

3 eggs

$^3/_4$ cup brown sugar

2 cups mashed cooked pumpkin

1 tablespoon cornstarch

$1^1/_4$ teaspoons cinnamon

$^1/_2$ teaspoon ginger

$^1/_2$ teaspoon nutmeg

$^1/_4$ teaspoon cloves

$^1/_4$ teaspoon salt

$1^1/_4$ cups milk

1 6-ounce can evaporated milk

$^1/_2$ cup chopped pecans

$^1/_4$ cup brown sugar, firmly packed

$^1/_4$ cup butter or margarine, melted

Prepare your favorite unbaked pie crust (filling is generous—crimp edges high).

Preheat oven to 400°. Beat eggs slightly in large bowl, add brown sugar, pumpkin, cornstarch, spices, and salt, mix well. Stir in milk and evaporated milk. Pour into pastry shell. Bake for 20 minutes.

Combine chopped pecans, brown sugar, and melted butter. Sprinkle mixture over pie. Continue to bake another 20 minutes or until knife inserted halfway between center and edge comes out clean. Cool on wire rack about $1^1/_2$ hours.

Mildred Howie
Healdsburg, CA

SINLESS PUMPKIN PIE

Heat oven to 350°. Spray 9-inch pie pan with non-stick cooking spray. In a blender, mix all ingredients until completely mixed, stirring occasionally. When mixed, pour into pie pan and bake for 50 minutes, turning once during baking.

Bob Carter
Oxnard, CA

 Here's an easy-to-make pie that's low in fat and sugar. This delicious finale to any meal makes its own crust. For added flavor, top each serving with 1 tablespoon of lite whipped topping before serving.

1 12-ounce can lite evaporated skimmed milk

1 16-ounce can solid pack pumpkin

1 egg

2 egg whites

$^1\!/_2$ cup biscuit mix

2 tablespoons sugar

1 tablespoon granulated sugar substitute

1 teaspoon ground cinnamon

$^1\!/_2$ teaspoon ground nutmeg

$^1\!/_8$ teaspoon ground allspice

$^1\!/_4$ teaspoon ground ginger

$2^1\!/_2$ teaspoons vanilla

PUMPKIN SOUP

1 pound meaty short ribs

4 cups water

1 8-ounce can pumpkin or about
3 cups fresh pumpkin,
cut up and cubed

1 potato, peeled, quartered

1 large carrot, quartered

1 medium onion, quartered

salt to taste

$1/4$ teaspoon white pepper

$1/2$ cup light cream

Brown short ribs over low heat in 4-quart Dutch oven. Add water, simmer for 1 hour. Remove ribs, cut meat from bones and return to broth. Add pumpkin, potato, carrot, onion, salt, and pepper. Simmer 45 minutes.

Pour $1/3$ of mixture into food processor, blend until smooth, repeat until all has been puréed. Heat well and serve in bowls with a little cream on top of each bowl. Do not stir before serving.

Chef Maxine Cathcart, monthly food columnist
The Valley Reporter
Yucaipa, CA

PUMPKIN FEST STEW

Sauté onions, carrots, garlic, cumin, and curry powder in oil in large saucepot over medium heat. Add small amount of broth, as necessary, to prevent sticking. Stir frequently for about 5 minutes, until onion is translucent. Add lentils, tomatoes, and broth. Cover and bring to a boil. Then, lower heat and simmer for 15 minutes.

Add pumpkin, increase heat, and bring to a boil. Then, reduce heat and simmer, covered, for 30 minutes, until lentils and pumpkin are tender. Season with salt and pepper to taste.

Gail Hobbs
Author, *Soup's On! Hot Recipes from Cool Chefs*
Ventura, CA

2 large yellow onions, chopped

2 large carrots, sliced thin

2 tablespoons crushed garlic

1 tablespoon cumin

1 tablespoon curry powder

1 cup lentils

1 32-ounce can chopped tomatoes with juice

2 cups vegetable broth

2 pounds fresh pumpkin, peeled and cubed

salt and freshly ground black pepper to taste

SALMON FESTIVAL

KLAMATH

Annual. Third weekend in August.

36

For more than thirty years, the Klamath Salmon Festival and the Yurok Indian Tribe have worked hand-in-hand to celebrate the mighty salmon and highlight the importance of Native American and Yurok culture.

The weekend begins with a parade in the morning and events continue throughout the weekend, with entertainment featured at the stage area. Entertainment activities include demonstrations of Yurok dance, drums, and singing. Exhibit booths include Yurok Tribe culture and history. A dazzling array of Indian wares are sold and displayed by Native American arts and crafts vendors from all over California. Look for Yurok shell and bead jewelry.

Ceremonies and competitions include the crowning of the winners of the Na-Re-Wolth Wa'Eyon and Che-Nec contests. The winners are crowned with beaded headbands of traditional Yurok basket designs. The Logging Show features both professionals and amateurs taking part in the hot saw, choker setting, ax throw, double bucking, and the obstacle pole rivalry. Who knows, you may want to try your hand by participating in a few of the contests.

Kids are given the opportunity to participate in special activities that revolve around Native American life. They'll be fascinated to learn about Indian life and times as they take part in hands-on pursuits.

The major highlight of the Salmon Festival, however, is the traditional salmon dinner held along the Klamath River. The meal features salmon cooked in the traditional Yurok manner. This culinary treat provides an opportunity for everyone attending the celebration to enjoy one of the world's finest and most nutritious seafoods.

YUROK-STYLE BARBECUED SALMON

Prepare barbecue pit in sand. Use only dried alder or madrone to make fire. Lightly sprinkle fillets with garlic salt and lemon pepper. Place on smoothed redwood spears. When fire is hot, arrange speared salmon fillets around pit in an oblong fashion. Turn fillets as necessary to cook both sides.

Yurok Tribe
Klamath, CA

Chinook salmon fillets

lemon pepper

garlic salt

dried alder or madrone wood for fire

prepared redwood spear sticks

LINDA'S SALMON PARTY LOG

2 cups cooked salmon

8 ounces cream cheese, softened

2 tablespoons lemon juice

2 tablespoons very finely chopped
onion

1 large teaspoon of prepared
horseradish

$1/4$ teaspoon salt

$1/4$ teaspoon liquid smoke

$1/2$ cup chopped pecans

3 tablespoons coarsely snipped
parsley

Drain and flake salmon, removing any skin or bones. Combine salmon with cream cheese, lemon juice, onion, horseradish, salt, and liquid smoke, mix thoroughly. Chill several hours or overnight. Shape salmon mixture into an 8x2-inch log, chill well. Mix pecans and parsley (may be kept in refrigerator prior to rolling on log). Roll salmon log in mixture and chill for another two hours. Serve with Triscuits or crackers of your choice.

Yurok Tribe
Klamath, CA

CALIFORNIA SALMON QUICHE

Layer potato slices in pie crust, then add flaked salmon. Mix remaining ingredients in mixing bowl and pour carefully over pie. Bake in 325° oven for 25 to 30 minutes, or until knife blade comes out clean. Serve at room temperature or chilled.

California Salmon Council
Folsom, CA

3 large potatoes, sliced

1 pie crust (9-inch pie pan)

1 cup cooked, flaked salmon

2 eggs (or 3 egg whites or equivalent egg substitute)

$1/2$ cup nonfat milk

1 cup nonfat cottage cheese

2 tablespoons chopped dill (preferably fresh)

$1/4$ teaspoon salt

$1/4$ teaspoon pepper

CALIFORNIA SALMON TOSTADAS

6 tostada shells, or 6 corn tortillas, crisped in hot oil or oven

1½ cups cooked white rice, mixed with salt, pepper and juice of 1 lime

1 pound salmon, poached, flaked (or any white fish)

1 cup chopped cucumber

1 cup chopped bell pepper (red, yellow, or green in any combination)

1 head romaine lettuce, shredded

½ bunch cilantro, finely chopped

Guacamole

2 ripe avocadoes, cubed

2 large tomatoes, diced

2 large red onions, finely chopped

1 bulb garlic, minced

2 jalapeño or serrano chilies, minced

½ teaspoon cumin

½ teaspoon oregano

salt and pepper to taste

juice of 2 limes

Garnish

½ cup black olives, sliced

1 cup low fat sour cream or yogurt

lime wedges

chilies

On each plate, place tostada shell and spread on some rice. Layer salmon, vegetables, lettuce, and cilantro. Garnish with guacamole, olives, sour cream or yogurt, and lime wedges.

Guacamole: Mix all ingredients, chill before serving.

California Salmon Festival
Klamath, CA

SEAFOOD, ART & WINE FESTIVAL

BODEGA BAY

Annual. August date varies.

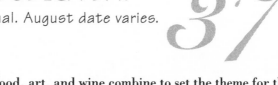

37

Seafood, art, and wine combine to set the theme for this weekend festival. You'll experience a mouth-watering variety of delectable dishes from which to choose. There are shrimp and vegetable kabobs, Cajun seafood gumbo, barbecued oysters, grilled albacore, and more. Think of it, you can even take along alligator-on-a-stick as you visit the colorful arts and crafts market. American alligator meat is increasing in popularity as a kitchen meat staple. It has a unique flavor that is enhanced by seasonings and sauces. The taste compares favorably to pork and chicken. When you feel the need to wash down some of the dining delectables, you'll discover superb wine and microbrewed beer from local vintners and brewers.

The vendor market gives festival patrons a chance to see and buy fine works from artists and crafters from throughout California. This festival prides itself on the quality of its artists.

Entertainment areas feature music and fun for children and adults. Two stages are filled with entertainers, including jugglers, a children's chorus, and other assorted treats. Youngters can also enjoy a petting zoo and pony rides.

The small town of Bodega sometimes gets overlooked by travelers who journey along California Highway 1. Bodega is located an easy 5 miles east of the highway. Bodega and nearby Bodega Bay were made famous by Alfred Hitchcock's film, *The Birds.*

GRILLED ALBACORE STEAKS

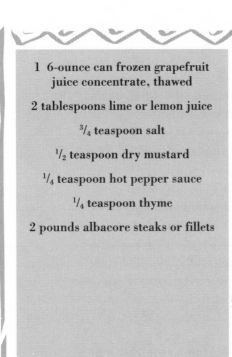

1 6-ounce can frozen grapefruit
   juice concentrate, thawed

2 tablespoons lime or lemon juice

$^3/_4$ teaspoon salt

$^1/_2$ teaspoon dry mustard

$^1/_4$ teaspoon hot pepper sauce

$^1/_4$ teaspoon thyme

2 pounds albacore steaks or fillets

Combine grapefruit juice concentrate, lemon juice, salt, dry mustard, hot pepper sauce, and thyme in small bowl. Place fish on hot grill and baste with sauce. Cook 5 minutes, turn, baste again, cook an additional 5 minutes.

Terry Poland
Oxnard, CA

 Try preparing this dish over a campfire barbecue for unbelievable results.

CRAB & BRIE LOAF

Cut a "lid" from the top of the bread and remove the inside of the bread, forming a basket about ½ inch thick on the sides and bottom. Cube the removed bread. Mix the butter and garlic together and rub it over the inside and outside of the bread basket and lid. Remove rind from cheese. Cut cheese into chunks to lay evenly in the bottom of the basket. Top with crabmeat, sprinkle with nuts, and cover with bread lid. Arrange the cheese-filled basket and bread cubes on a foil-lined baking sheet. Bake in a 350° oven for about 10 minutes until the bread cubes are toasted. Remove the cubes and continue baking for 10 to 15 minutes until the cheese is melted and the outside of bread basket is crispy.

Gail Hobbs, author
A Sizzling Affair newsletter
Ventura, CA

8-ounce round French or
sourdough bread loaf

2 tablespoons butter, softened

1 tablespoon garlic, minced

4 ounces brie

4 ounces crabmeat

½ cup chopped pecans

CALIFORNIA SWORDFISH CEVICHE

12 ounces California swordfish, skin and dark meat removed

1 cup freshly squeezed lime juice for marinade

1 small red onion, diced

2 medium tomatoes, cored, seeded, and diced

$1/2$ cup freshly squeezed orange juice

$1/2$ cup tomato juice

1 tablespoon freshly squeezed lime juice

$1^1/2$ jalapeños, stems and seeds removed, finely chopped

1 bunch fresh oregano leaves, chopped

$1/4$ cup olive oil

$1/2$ cup small green olives

1 teaspoon salt

$1/2$ teaspoon freshly ground black pepper

3 bay leaves

Cut swordfish into $1/2$-inch squares. Place the fish in a non-metallic container and add the lime juice. Marinate in the refrigerator for 30 minutes. Drain the fish, discarding the lime juice. Transfer fish to a bowl.

Add the remaining ingredients, toss well, and let sit for 1 hour (or up to overnight) in the refrigerator. Remove bay leaves. Serve cold in chilled glasses or on lettuce-lined plates with crispy fried corn tortilla chips to accompany.

Chefs Susan Feniger and Mary Sue Milliken
California Seafood Council
Santa Barbara, CA

SNOWFEST!
LAKE TAHOE

Annual. Seasonal. Typically the first 10 days of March.

Imagine yourself surrounded by snow-capped mountains, a crystal clear lake, and enough feasting and fun to fill a lifetime. That's what you'll discover when you join the excitement and entertainment of Snowfest!, North Lake Tahoe and Truckee's premier winter carnival.

The North Tahoe and Truckee winter carnival showcases America's greatest concentration of skiing during ten full days of special events. You'll discover the most delicious Snowfest! event is the Wild Game & Fish Cook-off. That's where local restaurants offer unique and delectable dishes consisting of wild game. You'll have a chance to savor duck, venison, fish, and even bear as you join the other tasters feasting at the cook-off.

But wait, there's more. Snowfest! offers one hundred and twenty separate events, including skiing, children's activities, parades, fireworks, gourmet delights, live entertainment, dancing, contests, theater, and a whole lot more.

Lake Tahoe is the largest alpine lake on the North American continent and one of California's premier destinations. Interestingly, the water in Lake Tahoe is so clear that a dinner plate can be visible at seventy-five feet below the surface. Lake Tahoe is twenty-two miles long and twelve miles wide. It's located about 200 miles northeast of San Francisco, 98 miles northeast of Sacramento, and 58 miles southwest of Reno, Nevada.

LAKE TAHOE CRAB CAKES

1 pound lump crabmeat, cleaned

1 teaspoon chopped parsley

1 teaspoon lemon juice

2 tablespoons finely diced
red peppers

2 tablespoons finely diced
green peppers

1 teaspoon Old Bay seasoning

2 teaspoons heavy cream

4 teaspoons bread crumbs

$\frac{1}{2}$ teaspoon salt

$\frac{1}{2}$ teaspoon white pepper

1 teaspoon chopped garlic

$\frac{1}{2}$ teaspoon Worcestershire sauce

1 egg

Pick all shell out of crab. Mix all ingredients together. Shape into cakes, approximately 3 ounces each. Refrigerate until ready to use. Sauté in a teflon-coated pan until brown on one side, flip and place into an ovenproof baking dish. Bake in a hot oven for 4 to 6 minutes, until hot and cooked through. Serve immediately with tartar sauce.

Executive Chef Ian Orr
Caesars Tahoe
Lake Tahoe, CA

SNOW ICE CREAM

Mix all ingredients until an ice cream consistency is achieved. Variations: add other flavors, fruits, chocolate chips, nuts, or shredded coconut.

Rick Page
Kansas City, MO

2 quarts fresh snow (powder)

$1/3$ cup sugar

1 teaspoon vanilla

1 pinch salt

$1/3$ cup cream or half-and-half

VENISON CHOPS

4 or 5 deer chops

flour

salt and pepper (use extra pepper)

5 or 6 slices bacon

1 tablespoon shortening

liquid gravy bouquet

Rinse and pat dry the chops, dredge in flour seasoned with salt and pepper—use extra pepper. Fry bacon, reserve bacon grease. Crumble bacon strips and set aside. Add 1 tablespoon shortening to bacon grease. When grease is medium hot, add dredged chops, cover with lid. Cook completely and brown on first side. Turn and brown other side. Chops are usually thin and cook quickly. Remove chops to a platter and sprinkle with bacon crumbs.

For gravy, make a base of flour, salt, and pepper. Brown in bacon grease. Add water for texture and one capful of gravy bouquet for flavor and coloring. Add extra pepper. The gravy will be dark and rich.

Patty and Joe Fessenden
Mission, TX

BEAR ROAST

Rinse roast well. Place in baking dish, add pepper, cover with bacon strips and foil. Cook 6 hours at 300°. Check for tenderness. You should be able to cut roast with a fork.

Using the pan liquid, make a thick gravy using a paste of flour, salt, and pepper. Add gravy bouquet, extra pepper, and additional water if necessary.

Patty and Joe Fessenden
Mission, TX

 All wild meat can be enhanced with extra pepper before cooking.

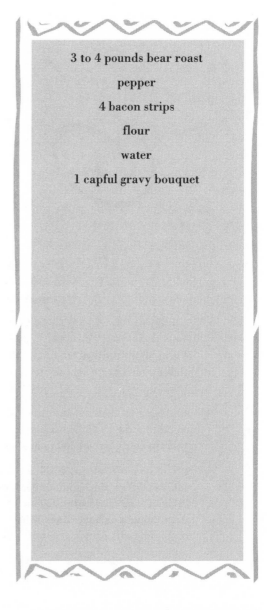

3 to 4 pounds bear roast

pepper

4 bacon strips

flour

water

1 capful gravy bouquet

SOLAR COOK-OFF

TAYLORSVILLE

Annual. Saturday following July 4th.

Are you a gourmet who's bored with the same old menu and preparation techniques? There's nothing quite like the Solar Cook-Off. It is a celebration of the community, alternative energy, and the environment. As the world approaches the next millennium, many folks begin to take a new look at conserving, recycling, and making better use of limited resources. If that's all new to you, this event will educate, surprise, and entertain you, and at the same time open a world of alternative feastings.

According to organizers of this unique event, it's a grassroots, eclectic group of individuals who make this celebration special and set it apart.

You'll discover the Taylorsville Rodeo Grounds filled with plenty of simple and sensational food and refreshments, solar-cooked food, and solar energy demonstrations. Throughout the day, a line-up of solar-energized musicians rotate playing swing-style classics, acoustic rock, western tunes, funky rhythms, and butt-rockin' blues.

Throughout the day, people bring their ovens and cook whatever they want. They share satisfying food and refreshing recipes with other solar cooks and usually with interested members of the public. Vegetarian solar cooking is sold by the local food cooperative, and awesome barbecued food is provided by local vendors.

If you haven't yet tasted solar-cooked food, here's your chance. You'll find thirty to fifty solar ovens scattered about cooking up tasty delights—everything from soup, appetizers, lasagna, and casseroles, to whole turkeys. If you prefer, you're invited to bring your own store-bought or homemade solar oven and spend the day cooking up a storm amid solar chefs, friendly people, exuberant entertainment, and high-performance solar ovens.

You may want to stick around for an evening of dancing under the rays of the moon. But, buy your dance ticket early because it's usually sold out in advance.

Taylorsville is located on County Highway 23, a short distance from California Highway 70 in Plumas County.

According to Bill and Melody Rockett, "Everyone should experiment with sunstove cooking. The more people try it, the more they like it." The Rocketts helped organize the Solar Cook-Off from their Blackhawk Solar Access store in Taylorsville. They supplied all of the recipes for the Solar Cook-Off section.

BRAZILIAN BLACK BEAN SOUP

1½ cups dried black beans

1 onion, minced

1 clove garlic, finely minced
or crushed

1¾ pounds lean pork or beef,
cut in 2 inch pieces

¾ pound chorizo
(a garlic- seasoned sausage)

2 slices bacon, cubed

½ cup orange juice

½ cup red wine (optional)

chili pepper and salt to taste

orange slices for garnish

Soak beans overnight. Drain and cover with fresh water. Add onion and garlic. Cook in a covered pot for at least 2 hours.

Place pork or beef, sausage (left whole), and bacon in small amount of water and bring to a boil. Simmer for 5 minutes. Add meats to the beans and simmer for another 2 hours. Add orange juice and wine. Simmer for an additional 30 minutes. Remove sausage and slice in ½-inch rounds. Save some rounds for decoration, returning the remainder to the pot. Correct seasoning and stir. Serve on a bed of rice and decorate the beans with slices of oranges and sausage.

This dish is ideal for the sunstove because of the long slow-cooking time requirement.

WHITE BEAN SOUP

Combine beans, water, salt, bay leaf, thyme, onion, carrot, and celery in a pot. Simmer for about 3 hours under cover, or until beans are very tender. Remove from sunstove. Discard carrot, celery, and bay leaf. Drain and reserve liquid. Mash or force the beans through a sieve. Stir in reserved cooking liquid and add milk. Correct seasoning. Reheat the purée in the sunstove. Before serving this soup, add small pieces of butter and blend well.

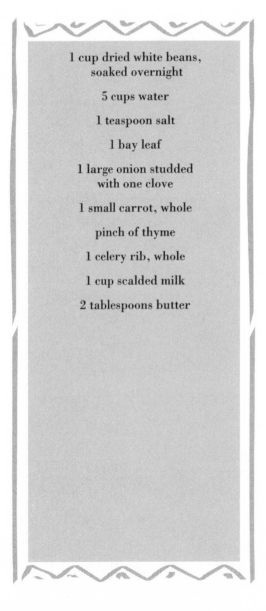

1 cup dried white beans,
soaked overnight

5 cups water

1 teaspoon salt

1 bay leaf

1 large onion studded
with one clove

1 small carrot, whole

pinch of thyme

1 celery rib, whole

1 cup scalded milk

2 tablespoons butter

CHEESECAKE

Crust

¹/₂ cup crushed graham crackers

2 tablespoons sugar

2 tablespoons butter

Filling

grated peel of 1 lemon

grated peel of ¹/₂ orange

¹/₂ teaspoon vanilla

³/₄ pound cream cheese

¹/₄ cup heavy cream

5 tablespoons sugar

2 large eggs

2 tablespoons sour cream

1 tablespoon milk

For crust, mix graham crackers with sugar and butter. Pat into an 8-inch pie pan and bake for about 15 minutes. Set aside and cool.

To prepare filling, add cream cheese to grated lemon, orange rind, and vanilla, beating well. Gradually add heavy cream and sugar, beating constantly. Add eggs, 1 at a time, beating well after each addition. Beat in sour cream and milk. Continue beating but avoid incorporating air into the mixture.

Pour cheese mixture into prepared pie pan and smooth the surface. Cover with black lid and bake in sunstove until center does not quiver when pan is shaken. Remove from oven and let stand for 10 minutes on rack. Invert and unmold while hot. Let stand until cool before serving.

The original recipe for this delicious cheesecake requires that the pie be placed in the oven and baked in a warm water bath. When baked in the sunstove this step is not necessary.

BANANA FLUFF

Fold mashed bananas carefully into whipped egg whites. Turn into well-buttered dish, cover, and sunbake for about 1 hour or until center becomes firm.

4 bananas, mashed

4 egg whites, beaten hard with a dash of salt and a few drops of lemon juice

TIMBERFEST

SIERRA COUNTY
Annual. Labor Day Weekend.

If you love great tasting ribs, and plenty of them, this is your kind of festival. The Sierra Timberfest is a countywide salute to the timber industry, its families, and fine cooked ribs.

The sizzling food is just the beginning of this rousing weekend of activities. Things start off on Friday with the Logger & Cowboy Poetry and Music Show. Early Saturday morning, more than fifty different big rigs, trucks, and cars travel through the area's communities showing support for the forest product industry and its families.

Following the Yellow Ribbon Rally, the heated competition begins among the area's best rib chefs and cooks. The competition is keen, the cooking is hearty, and the food is rib-ticklingly robust. The good folks from around the county take their rib cooking seriously, so you have a chance to taste some of the best ribs around. In addition to the ribs, be sure to start Sunday morning with the local Fire Department's pancake breakfast. It features gin fizzes and mounds of freshly prepared pancakes.

Throughout the weekend you'll find crowds of spectators on their feet, cheering for their favorite teams competing in tug-of-war games, log loading, knot bumping, and choker setting.

You don't want to miss the antique logging and equipment displays, arts and crafts, entertainment, and forestry exhibits. Saturday night, you're invited to join the dancers on the Little League field to dance the night away, howl at the moon, or just enjoy the sounds of one of the popular bands.

Sierra County is located in the heart of the northern section of the Sierra Nevada. The western half of the county is situated in the Sierra Buttes, an awesome range of peaks, waterfalls, and rivers. The eastern part is considered some of the finest farm and cattle ranch land in California. The festival is held in the town of Loyalton, 40 miles west of Reno, Nevada.

CHERRY DELICIOUS RIBS

8 pounds pork spareribs

$^1/_2$ cup chopped onion

2 tablespoons olive oil

1 21-ounce can cherry filling and topping

$^1/_4$ cup soy sauce

2 teaspoons spicy brown mustard

1 teaspoon ground ginger

1 teaspoon Worcestershire sauce

Cut ribs into serving portions of 2 or 3 ribs each. In a large saucepot or Dutch oven, simmer ribs, covered, in salted water for 45 to 50 minutes, or until tender. Drain.

In a large saucepan, cook onion in olive oil until tender. In an electric blender or food processor, purée cherry filling until smooth. Add filling, soy sauce, mustard, ginger, and Worcestershire sauce to onion mixture and mix well. Simmer, uncovered, for 10 to 15 minutes, stirring occasionally.

Place ribs on gas grill over low heat or on charcoal grill 4 to 6 inches from slow coals. Turn ribs 3 or 4 times and brush frequently with sauce. Cook 25 minutes, or until tender. Discard any remaining sauce.

The Cherry Marketing Institute
Okemos, MI

SWEET AND SOUR PORK RIBS

Combine all ingredients except ribs in slow cooker and stir well. Cut pork rib rack into individual portions. Add ribs to cooker and mix well to coat. Cover and cook on low setting for 8 to 10 hours.

Don Hobbs
Ventura, CA

8-ounce can of pineapple chunks

$1/2$ cup barbecue sauce

$1/4$ cup soy sauce

$1/4$ cup sherry

$1/3$ cup brown sugar

2 teaspoons garlic, minced

$1/4$ teaspoon black pepper

2 pounds lean babyback pork ribs

GRILLED CALIFORNIA SHORT RIBS

1 cup Worcestershsire sauce

¼ cup white wine vinegar

2 tablespoons lemon juice

1 tablespoon garlic, minced

salt and pepper to taste

2 pounds beef short ribs

Mix first 5 ingredients together and pour over ribs. Marinate in refrigerator for 4 to 6 hours. Grill over low fire for 50 to 60 minutes until cooked through. Baste often with remaining marinade during cooking.

Terry Poland
Oxnard, CA

 Try cooking these over an open campfire.

WALNUT FESTIVAL

WALNUT CREEK

Annual. Third weekend in September.

Want to know about the Walnut Festival? Here are the facts of its interesting past in a nutshell. The first walnut festival was a celebration of the harvest of grapes and was actually called the Grape Festival. During the years of prohibition, grapes were replaced by walnuts as the cash crop of the area, and the vineyards became walnut groves. In 1939, the harvest celebration became known as the Walnut Festival.

Preceding the opening of the festival, it's great fun to watch the enthusiasm build as the Walnut Festival Twilight Parade travels down Main Street. Participants include floats, marching bands, drill teams, clowns, and classic and antique cars.

Diverse activities are held during the Walnut Festival. The Great Chef's Invitational Competition is a contest requiring the utilization of walnuts in the preparation of the recipes. Student chefs from Diablo Valley College prepare walnut-oriented recipes during the Student Chefs competition. You'll be able to pick up some tasty give-away recipes as you visit the various demonstrations and programs.

This popular celebration, with an annual attendance of nearly 50,000, is known for its entertainment for all ages, arts and crafts, a Great Chef's competition, and amusement rides. In addition, children's activities and the children's parade provide some exciting experiences for youngsters. Included on the festival's agenda are a volleyball tournament, plenty of tasty international foods, and a variety of fun games.

The Walnut Festival grounds are located at Heather Farm Park, on the corner of North San Carol and Ygnacio Valley Road.

TARATOR SAUCE

1 cup walnuts

2 cloves garlic, finely minced

6 tablespoons tahini, stirred well

$\frac{1}{4}$ cup or more lemon juice

cold water, for thinning

salt

black and cayenne pepper to taste

Combine walnuts and garlic in food processor fitted with steel blade. Pulse on and off until finely chopped. Add tahini and lemon juice and pulse to combine. Add enough water to thin to desired consistency. Season with salt and pepper. Serve with assorted crisp, raw vegetable pieces.

The Walnut Marketing Board
San Francisco, CA

 Tahini is a raw sesame paste.

BARBECUED WALNUTS

On 12-inch square of foil, combine walnuts, garlic, cumin, salt, and oil. Wrap and seal in foil packet. Grill about 10 minutes over medium-hot coals, turning occasionally. Use as a garnish, as a snack, or as an appetizer on toasted baguette slices spread with herbed goat cheese. To prepare indoors, bake foil-wrapped walnuts in a 425° oven for 10 to 15 minutes. Turn packet occasionally.

Walnut Festival Association
Walnut Creek, CA

$1\frac{1}{2}$ cups walnut halves or pieces

2 cloves garlic, peeled and chopped

$\frac{1}{2}$ teaspoon ground cumin

$\frac{1}{2}$ teaspoon salt

3 tablespoons olive oil

CHICKEN BREASTS WITH WALNUT ORANGE SAUCE

4 chicken breasts, skinned and boned

6 to 8 tablespoons butter

$1/4$ cup chopped walnuts

1 teaspoon orange zest

$1/4$ cup fresh orange juice

1 tablespoon brown sugar

1 green onion, chopped (green part only)

Cook chicken in a little butter over medium-high heat. Set chicken aside on a warm plate. To pan, add the rest of the butter, walnuts, orange zest, and orange juice. Cook for a minute and then add brown sugar and green onion and cook 1 to 2 minutes more. Stir while cooking down the orange juice. Once the sauce is done, pour over chicken and serve immediately.

Chef Dennis Mecum
First Place Winner, Firehouse Cooks Competition

SAVORY WALNUT SNACKS

Coat a large, shallow baking pan with non-stick vegetable spray. Mix egg whites with spices. Stir in walnuts and coat thoroughly. Spread in pan, bake at 350° for 15 to 18 minutes, until dry and crisp. Microwave directions: Cook on high in 4 or 5 batches for 2 to 3 minutes each. Cool before serving.

Walnut Festival Association
Walnut Creek, CA

This spiced nut recipe can be prepared in less than 5 minutes. It may be easily altered to impart a variety of flavors, both sweet and savory.

2 egg whites, slightly beaten

1½ teaspoons ground
cayenne pepper

1 tablespoon chili powder

2 teaspoons ground cumin

2 teaspoons salt

4 cups (1 pound) shelled walnuts

WHALE FESTIVAL
FORT BRAGG
Annual. Third Saturday in March.

42

No, they don't serve whale. This festival does, however, provide some wonderfully tasty seafood, with brews to wash it down.

The annual migration of the California gray whale is reason for celebration in Fort Bragg. As the gargantuan mammals pass along the Mendocino coastline, they're welcomed with a special festival in their honor.

During the festivities, you can sample specialty brews from several of Northern California's leading microbrewers, take a whale of a run and walk during the 10K run and 5K walk, discover some handy hints and easy recipes, feast on tasty food prepared by local chefs, and shop for wares offered by local artisans. Mindy, a 42-foot gray whale model with movable parts, is on exhibit the entire weekend. In addition, you can browse through a gem and mineral show, plus a sports card and comic book show and sale. By the way, don't forget to cast a vote for your favorite seafood chowder prepared by the Mendocino coast's great chefs.

The real excitement is provided when you stop and observe, up-close, the natural beauty of the whales as they breach, spy-hop, and spout their way along the California coastline.

Fort Bragg is located 150 miles north of San Francisco, on the Mendocino coast. The town was founded in 1857 as a military post. Ten years later the installation was abandoned and lumber mills and commercial fishing began to develop.

SEAFOOD RED CHOWDER

Blend and heat tomatoes with juice, tomato sauce, and clam juice. Sauté celery, onion, and garlic in butter until golden brown. Add to tomato broth and simmer for 30 minutes. Add the seafood to chowder and simmer on low heat until seafood is cooked.

The Pasta House
Fort Bragg, CA

1 16-ounce can tomatoes,
diced, with juice

1 16-ounce can tomato sauce

1 16-ounce can sea clams, with juice

2 celery stalks, chopped

1 yellow onion, chopped

1 tablespoon minced garlic

butter

16 ounces scallops

16 ounces baby shrimp

SEAFOOD CHOWDER

1 cup chopped celery

1 cup chopped white onions

$\frac{1}{4}$ cup minced garlic

$\frac{1}{4}$ cup minced shallots

$\frac{1}{2}$ cup butter

1 cup Madeira wine

1 tablespoon coarse black pepper

$\frac{1}{2}$ tablespoon white ground pepper

$\frac{1}{4}$ teaspoon red pepper flakes

$\frac{1}{4}$ cup chopped fresh dill

6 large Yukon gold potatoes,
cut in large pieces

1 8-ounce bottle clam juice

$1\frac{1}{2}$ cups diced bacon

1 pound fresh rock shrimp

1 pound fresh sea scallops

1 pound fresh swordfish

1 pound fresh halibut

2 cans baby clams

2 cups heavy cream

Sauté celery, onions, garlic, and shallots in butter for 10 minutes over medium heat. Add wine, peppers, and dill. Add seafood, except for clams. Cover and let simmer for 10 to 15 minutes. Cook potatoes in the clam juice over medium heat until tender. Sauté bacon until crisp, strain off fat and add bacon to the potatoes. Add baby clams. Mix everything together. Add cream and heat but do not boil.

Little River Inn
Little River, CA

FLOUNDER FILLETS DIJON

Combine carrots, parsley, oil, salt, and pepper in a 7x11x2-inch microwave-safe baking dish. Cover with wax paper. Microwave at 100-percent power 5 minutes, stirring once.

To make an even thickness, fold over thin fillets or bend long fillets. Place fillets on top of carrots in the corners of the dish with the thick parts toward the outside and the thin parts toward the center. Combine the mustard and honey, spread over fillets. Cover with wax paper, microwave at 100-percent power 2 minutes. Rotate fillets, placing cooked parts toward the center and continue to cook 1 to 3 minutes longer or just until fish flakes easily when tested with a fork. Let stand, covered, for 2 minutes. Arrange fish and carrots on warm plates.

National Fisheries Institute
Arlington, VA

4 large carrots, julienned

2 tablespoons parsley, minced

1 teaspoon olive oil

$1/8$ teaspoon salt

$1/8$ teaspoon pepper

4 4- to 5-ounce fillets of flounder, tilapia, sole, cod, catfish, halibut, ocean perch, trout, orange roughy, or pollack

2 teaspoons coarse-grain Dijon mustard

1 teaspoon honey

ZUCCHINI FESTIVAL

ANGELS CAMP

Annual. Third Saturday in September.

43

There are 86,400 seconds in a day. Why not spend some of them celebrating the zucchini? Why a Zucchini Festival in Angels Camp? It's to pay tribute to the county's most popular squash.

Held in Utica Park, the fun-filled, family festival honors the vegetable by holding a Zucchini Derby, Zucchini Catapult, and a Zuke Ball. The park is filled with arts, crafts, and food booths. Food vendors are asked to be as creative as possible and to feature a Zucchini Zpecialty on their menu. Entertainment takes place all day long.

A smorgasbord of activities occurs during the zany zucchini event. Local master gardeners hold informational workshops and spotlight gardening techniques unique to the Mother Lode area. Since zucchini can grow almost anywhere, you'll learn helpful tips and techniques to have your own successful zucchini patch at home. You might want to consider entering the Zucchini Bonnet competition. The only requirement is that each chapeau must incorporate a zucchini. The contest is open to both adults and kids. Other featured events include the Zuke-Creature and Zukemobile competitions.

Angels Camp is nestled in the foothills of the Sierra Nevada, approximately 55 miles east of the city of Stockton. Founded during the gold rush of the 1800s, it's considered one of the Mother Lode's most historic towns.

ZUCCHINI PANCAKES

Pat the grated zucchini with paper towels to dry. Gently press out excess moisture. In mixing bowl, combine all ingredients except oil. Heat oil in skillet. Drop batter into hot oil with large serving spoon. Flatten with spatula. Fry until golden brown on both sides. As each batch is cooked, hold in warm oven on plate lined with a paper towel.

Mildred Howie
Healdsburg, CA

4 medium zucchini, coarsely grated

$1/2$ chopped sweet onion

1 clove minced garlic

2 beaten eggs

2 teaspoons flour

a pinch or two of chopped parsley

2 tablespoons grated
Parmesan cheese

5 teaspoons olive oil

ITALIAN ZUCCHINI BAKE

1 cup biscuit mix

3 tablespoons chopped fresh oregeno

$1/2$ cup grated Parmesan cheese

salt and pepper to taste

2 or 3 garlic cloves, puréed

3 strips bacon, fried and crumbled

$1/2$ cup chopped onion

2 cups sliced zucchini

4 eggs, slightly beaten

$1/4$ cup oil

grated mozzarella or Monterey Jack cheese (topping)

Mix together biscuit mix, oregano, Parmesan cheese, salt, and pepper. Add garlic and bacon. Stir in onion and zucchini. Mix in eggs and oil. Pour into greased 8x12-inch pan. Top with cheese. Bake 30 minutes in 350° oven.

Daisy Riley
West Point, CA

ZUCCHINI TOMATO CASSEROLE

Wash and slice zucchini, peel and slice tomatoes and onion, divide onion into rings. In 3-quart oiled casserole, place a layer of zucchini, tomato, and onion rings. Sprinkle on a little salt, pepper, brown sugar, and basil. Add a handful of crumbs, a few bits of butter, and a handful of cheese. Repeat twice, ending with cheese. Bake, covered, a total of 1¼ hours at 350°. Remove lid after ½ hour and finish baking.

Maxine Cathcart
Valley Messenger columnist and author of *Cuisine by Maxine*
Yucaipa, CA

12 small zucchini

12 small tomatoes

1 very large onion

salt and pepper to taste

brown sugar to taste

1 teaspoon basil

1½ cups soda cracker crumbs

1 stick butter

1½ cups grated cheddar cheese

ZUCCHINI CAKE

4 cups sifted flour

3 cups sugar

1 cup brown sugar

3 teaspoons baking soda

3 teaspoons baking powder

2 teaspoons cinnamon

1 teaspoon salt

5 eggs

1¼ cups vegetable oil

2 cups grated zucchini

1 banana, mashed

1 grated orange peel

2 teaspoons rum

1 cup chopped walnuts

Sift flour, sugars, baking soda, baking powder, cinnamon, and salt together. Beat eggs until foamy. Add oil and beat for a few seconds. Add zucchini, banana, and orange peel, beating well after each addition. Combine with dry ingredients. Add rum and walnuts.

Grease and flour cake pan or three small loaf pans. Spoon batter into pan and spread evenly. Bake in 350° oven for approximately 40 minutes, or until a wooden toothpick inserted in center comes out clean.

Mary Mazzia
Angels Camp, CA

FURTHER FEASTINGS

The following selected food and wine events are among those held in Northern California not included in the main section of this book. To obtain a complimentary copy of "California Celebrations," contact the California Division of Tourism, P.O. Box 1499, Sacramento 95812. To receive information regarding special events held in each community, write or call the city chamber of commerce and/or visitor centers.

January

Carrot Festival (Holtville) 619-356-2923. Food, parade, entertainment, arts and crafts.

Crab, Wine & Art Festival (Eureka) 707-442-6441; fax 707-442-0637. Food, wine tasting, art exhibits.

February

World Championship Crab Races (Crescent City) 800-343-8300 or 707-464-3174. Food, entertainment, children's activities, crab races.

March

Celtic Faire (Sonora) 800-446-1333 or 209-532-8375; fax 209-533-0956. Food, entertainment, arts and crafts, games.

Irish Days (Murphys) 800-225-3764 or 209-728-8517. Food, parade, entertainment, arts and crafts.

Taste of Main Street (Eureka) 707-442-9054. Food, tastings, entertainment.

April

Apple Blossom Festival (Sebastopol) 707-824-0501. Food, parade, entertainment, children's activities, cooking demonstrations.

Butter & Egg Days Parade (Petaluma) 707-762-2793; fax 707-762-4721. Food, parade, entertainment, children's activities.

Cherry Blossom Festival (San Francisco) 415-563-2313. Food, parade, entertainment, arts and crafts.

Chili Cook-off (Lakeport) 800-525-3743 or 707-263-5092.

Spring Wine Adventure (Lake County) 800-525-3743 or 707-279-8861. Food, brew tastings, cook-off.

May

Bebop & Brew (Arcata) 707-826-2207. Food, ale tastings, entertainment.

Cinco de Mayo Festival (San Jose) 408-258-0663. Food, parade, entertainment, arts and crafts.

Jewish Food Festival (Stockton) 209-477-9306. Food, entertainment, children's activities.

Strawberry Festival (Galt) 209-745-2529. Food, entertainment, growing demonstrations.

Wine Festival (Tiburon) 415-435-5633; fax 415-435-1132. Food, wine tastings, entertainment, silent auction.

June

Arts & Wine Festival (Foster City) 415-573-7600; fax 415-573-5201. Food, wine tastings, entertainment, arts and crafts.

Art & Wine Festival (San Anselmo) 415-454-2510; fax 415-258-9458. Food, wine tasting, entertainment, art exhibits.

Art & Wine Festival (Walnut Creek) 510-934-2007; fax 510-573-2404. Food, wine tastings, arts and crafts, children's activities, grape stomp.

Art & Wine in the Park (Fortuna) 707-725-9261; fax 707-725-3423. Food and wine tastings, entertainment, arts and crafts, children's activities, auctions.

Crawdad Festival (Isleton) 916-777-5880. Food, parade, arts and crafts, crawdad races.

Dairy Festival (Hilmar) 209-384-3333; fax 209-384-8472. Food, entertainment, arts and crafts, children's activities.

Rice Festival (Gridley) 916-846-3333. Food, arts and crafts, cooking demonstrations, farmers' market.

Scottish Highland Games & Gathering of the Clans (Modesto) 209-538-0821. Food, entertainment, competitions.

Wine & Food Renaissance (Lakeport) 800-525-3743 or 707-263-6658; fax 707-263-3933. Food and wine tastings, entertainment, auction.

July

Calpine Kit-n'-Caboodle Chili Cook-Off (Loyalton) 800-200-4949 or 916-993-6900. Food, entertainment, arts and crafts, children's activities, contests.

Connoisseur's Marketplace (Menlo Park) 415-325-2818; fax 415-325-0920. Food, wine and beer, entertainment, arts and crafts, children's activities.

Deep Pit Barbecue & Fireworks (Willow Creek) 916-629-2693. Food, entertainment, games.

August

Art & Wine Festival (Cupertino) 408-252-7054; fax 408-252-0638. Food, wine, arts and crafts, children's activities.

Gravenstein Apple Fair (Sebastopol) 707-829-4728. Food, wine, entertainment, arts and crafts.

Greek Food Festival (Sacramento) 916-443-2033; fax 916-443-2743. Food, entertainment, displays.

Japanese Cultural Bazaar (Sacramento) 916-446-0121; fax 916-446-1866. Food, entertainment, children's activities, flower arranging.

Plum Peachy Festival (Loomis) 916-652-7251. Food, entertainment, arts and crafts, farmers' market.

Round Valley Blackberry Festival (Covelo) 707-983-6736. Food, entertainment, arts and crafts.

Tomato Festival (Fairfield) 707-422-0103. Food, entertainment, arts and crafts, children's activities, farmers' market.

September

Apple Hill (Camino) 916-644-7692. Food, wine, arts and crafts, children's activities.

Blackberry & Bluegrass Festival (Mt. Shasta) 916-926-6212. Food, entertainment, concerts.

Grape Festival & Harvest Fair (Lodi) 209-369-2771; fax 209-369-9185. Food, entertainment, children's activities, competitions, grape stomp.

Indian Days (Fort Bragg) 800-726-2780 or 707-961-6300. Food, entertainment, arts and crafts, storytelling.

International Food Fair, 209-944-9347 or 209-465-3612. Food, entertainment, children's activities.

Octoberfest (Mammoth Lakes) 619-934-9451; fax 619-934-9716. Food, entertainment, contests.

Pasta Cook-off/Sausage Challenge (Weed) 916-938-4624. Food tastings, arts and crafts, farmers' market.

Sea Fest Bear Country Weekend (Crescent City) 707-464-0497. Food, parade, entertainment, arts and crafts.

October

Apple Harvest Festival (Fortuna) 707-725-2123.
Food, entertainment, contest, bake sale.

Great Halloween & Pumpkin Festival on Polk
(San Francisco) 415-346-4446; fax 415-346-0126.
Food, entertainment, arts and crafts.

Greek Festival (Eureka) 800-862-4906 or
707-442-6441; fax 707-442-0637. Food, wine,
entertainment.

Harvest Festival (Mt. Shasta) 916-926-6212.
Food, arts and crafts, entertainment, contests.

Harvest Festival (Pacific Grove) 408-373-3304;
fax 408-373-3317. Food, parade, entertainment,
arts and crafts, children's activities, contests.

Octoberfest (Lakeport) 800-525-3743 or
707-263-3222; fax 707-263-9564. Food,
entertainment, arts and crafts, children's activities.

Seafood Celebration (Benicia) 707-745-9791;
fax 707-745-9793. Food, wine and beer tastings,
children's activities.

November

Mountain Mandarin Festival (Newcastle)
916-663-1918. Food, entertainment, arts and crafts,
cooking demonstrations, contests.

December

Adobe Luminaria Fiesta (Petaluma) 707-762-4871.
Food, procession, entertainment, lighted luminaries.

NORTHERN CALIFORNIA: CERTIFIED FARMERS' MARKETS

California's agricultural products are recognized among the finest grown anywhere in the world. There's nothing quite like fresh-picked produce, field-grown flowers, and warm-from-the-oven baked goods. All these, and more, are available at local farmers' markets held in most counties and communities around the state.

The following selected farmers' markets are held in festival cities and counties included in this book. For additional information regarding these and other markets, contact area chambers of commerce and/or visitor centers.

Angels Camp
Bergantz parking lot, Wednesday, 3 P.M. to 7 P.M. (June-October), 209-736-4281.

Arcata
Arcata Plaza, Saturday, 9 A.M. to 1 P.M. (May-November), 707-441-9699.

Calaveras County
Arnold Cedar Center, Sunday, 10 A.M. to 1:30 P.M. (May-September), 209-728-8864.

Fort Bragg
Laurel & Franklin, Wednesday, 3:30 P.M. to 5:30 P.M. (May-October), 707-743-1726.

Gilroy
Monterey & 5th, Thursday, 3 P.M. to 8 P.M. (May-November), 408-842-6964.

Healdsburg
North & Vine, Saturday, 9 A.M. to noon; Tuesday, 4 P.M. to 6:30 P.M. (June-October), 707-431-1956.

Humboldt County
Eureka/Eureka Mall, Thursday, 10 A.M. to 1 P.M. (June-October), 707-441-9699.

Fortuna/Del's parking lot, Tuesday, 3 P.M. to 6 P.M. (June-October) 707-768-3342.

Kelseyville
Konocti Winery, Saturday, 8 A.M. to noon (May-October), 707-279-0662.

Lake Tahoe
American Legion Hall/Highway 50, Tuesday, 9 A.M. to 1 P.M., 916-621-4772.

Watermelon patch at Dollar Hill, Thursday, 8:30 A.M. to 2 P.M. (June-October), 916-823-6183.

Lodi
School & Oak, Thursday, 5:30 P.M. to 8:30 P.M., 209-368-6891.

Marin County
Corte Madera/Village Shopping Center, Wednesday, 2 P.M. to 6 P.M. (May-October), 415-456-FARM.

Novato/Novato Old Town, Tuesday, 4 P.M. to 8 P.M. (May-October), 415-456-FARM.

Mendocino
Mendocino/Howard Street, Friday, noon to 2 P.M. (May-October), 707-743-1726

Morgan Hill
Downtown/3rd & Monterey, Saturday, 8:30 A.M. to 12:30 P.M. (June-November), 408-779-5130.

Napa Valley
Napa Chef's/1st & Coombs, Friday, 4 P.M. to 8 P.M. (May-November), 707-252-7142.

Downtown/West Pearl parking lot, Tuesday, 7:30 A.M. to noon (May-November), 707-252-7142.

St. Helena Railroad Depot, Friday, 7:30 A.M. to 11:30 A.M. (May-November), 707-963-7343.

Oakland

Downtown/9th & Broadway, Friday, 8 A.M. to 2 P.M., 415-456-3276.

Jack London Square, Sunday, 10 A.M. to 2 P.M., 800-949-FARM.

Sacramento

8571 Sunset, Sunday, 9 A.M. to 5 P.M.; Monday-Saturday, 7:30 A.M. to 8 P.M., 916-967-6197.

Plaza Park/10th & J, Wednesday, 10 A.M. to 2 P.M. (May-December), 916-363-3663.

Florin Mall/65th St., Thursday, 8 A.M. to 11:30 A.M., 916-363-3663.

Roosevelt Park/9th & P, Tuesday, 10 A.M. to 2 P.M. (June-October), 916-363-3663.

K Street Mall/11th & K, Thursday, 5 P.M. to 9 P.M. (May-October), 916-363-3663.

Sunrise Mall, Saturday, 8 A.M. to noon, 916-363-3663.

Sacramento Center/8th & W, Sunday, 8 A.M. to noon, 916-363-3663.

Sacramento Country Club/El Camino & Watt, Tuesday, 8 A.M. to 11:30 A.M., 916-363-3663.

Elk Grove Village, Sunday ,8 A.M. to 11 A.M. (June-October), 916-363-3663.

San Francisco

Market & 7th, Wednesday & Sunday, 7 A.M. to 5 P.M., 510-528-6987.

100 Alemany Blvd., Saturday, 6 A.M. to 6 P.M., 415-647-9423.

Ferry Building, Saturday, 8 A.M. to 1:30 P.M. 510-528-6987.

San Rafael

Downtown/Cijos & 4th Street, Thursday, 6 P.M. to 9 P.M. (April-October), 415-457-2266.

Civic Center/Highway 101 & San Pedro, Thursday & Sunday, 8 A.M. to 1 P.M., 415-456-FARM.

Santa Cruz

Lincoln & Cedar, Wednesday, 2:30 P.M. to 6:30 P.M., 408-429-8433.

Sonoma County

Cloverdale/Broad & Cloverdale, Saturday, 9 A.M. to 11:30 A.M. (May-November), 707-894-4623.

Petaluma/Walnut Park, Saturday, 2 P.M. to 5 P.M. (June-November), 707-762-0344.

Santa Rosa/Veterans' Building, Wednesday & Saturday, 8:30 A.M. to noon, 707-523-0962.

Sebastopol/New Town Plaza, Sunday, 10 A.M. to 1 P.M. (June-October), 707-522-9305.

Sonoma/Sonoma Plaza, Tuesday, 5:30 P.M. to dusk, 707-538-7023.

Stockton

March & Pacific, Thursday, 9 A.M. to 1 P.M.; Sunday, 9 A.M. to 1 P.M., 209-943-1830.

Washington & El Dorado, Saturday, 7 A.M. to noon, 209-943-1830.

Vacaville

Downtown/Main Street, Saturday, 8 A.M. to noon, 415-456-3276.

Walnut Creek/Broadway & Lincoln, Sunday, 8 A.M. to 1 P.M., 510-945-2940.

Yuba City

Center & Plumas, Saturday, 8 A.M. to noon (May-September), 916-671-3346.

INFORMATION DIRECTORY

For information and details regarding special events, restaurants, lodging, shopping, and attractions contact the following:

A La Carte (Marin County)

Events West, 99 East Blithedale Avenue, Mill Valley 94941, 415-383-9378; fax 415-383-0614.

Marin County Convention & Visitors Bureau, Avenue of the Flags, San Rafael 94903; 415-472-7470; fax 415-499-3700.

A La Carte, A La Park (San Francisco)

Events West, 99 East Blithedale Avenue, Mill Valley 94941, 415-383-9378; fax 415-383-0614.

San Francisco Visitor Information Center, Hallidie Plaza, Lower Level, P.O. Box 429097, 900 Market Street, San Francisco 94142-9097; 415-391-2000.

Abalone Festival (Mendocino)

Van Damme State Park; P.O. Box 440; Mendocino 95460; 707-937-4016.

Apricot Fiesta (Patterson)

Patterson Apricot Fiesta, P.O. Box 442, Patterson 95363, 209-892-3118.

Patterson-Westley Chamber of Commerce, P.O. Box 365, Patterson 95363; 209-892-2821.

Art a la Carte (Mammoth Lakes)

Mono County Arts Council, P.O. Box 17323, Mammoth Lakes; 619-934-3342.

Mammoth Lakes Visitors Bureau, P.O. Box 48, Mammoth Lakes 93546; 619-934-2712 or 800-367-6572; fax 619-934-7066.

Art & Pumpkin Festival (Half Moon Bay)

Half Moon Bay Art & Pumpkin Festival, P.O. Box 274, Half Moon Bay 94019; 415-726-9652.

Half Moon Bay Coastside Chamber of Commerce, 225 South Cabrillo, Half Moon Bay 93230; 415-726-8380.

Asparagus Festival (Stockton)

Stockton/San Joaquin Convention & Visitors Bureau, 46 West Fremont Street, Stockton 95202; 800-350-1967 or 209-943-1987; fax 209-943-6235.

Autumn Food & Wine Jubilee (Squaw Valley)

Tahoe North Vistors & Convention Bureau, P.O. Box 5578, Tahoe City, 96145; 800-824-6348 or 916-583-3494.

Blackberry Festival (Lake County)

Lake County Marketing Program, 875 Lakeport Boulevard, Lakeport 95453; 800-525-3743 or 707-263-9544; fax 707-263-9564.

Cherry Blossom Festival (Lodi)

Lodi District Chamber of Commerce, 1330 South Ham Lane, Lodi 95242, 800-304-LODI or 209-367-7840; fax 209-334-0528.

Chili Cook-Off (Willow Creek)

Willow Creek Chamber of Commerce, P.O. Box 704, Willow Creek 95573; 916-629-2693.

Chocolate Festival (Oakdale)

Oakdale District Chamber of Commerce & Visitors Bureau, 590 North Yosemite Avenue, Oakdale 95361; 209-847-2244; fax 209-847-0826.

Clam Chowder Cook-Off (Santa Cruz)

Santa Cruz Seaside Company, 400 Beach Street, Santa Cruz 95060; 408-423-5590.

Santa Cruz County Conference & Visitors Council, 701 Front Street, Santa Cruz 95060; 800-833-3494 or 408-425-1234.

Coastal Christmas (Humboldt County)

Eureka/Humboldt County Convention and Visitors Bureau, 1034 Second Street, Eureka 95501; 800-346-3482 or 707-443-5115; fax 707-443-5115.

Dry Bean Festival (Tracy)

Greater Tracy Chamber of Commerce and Visitor's Bureau, 223 East 10th Street, Tracy 95376; 209-835-2131; fax 209-833-9526.

Eggplant Festival (Loomis)

Loomis Basin Chamber of Commerce, P.O. Box 1212, Loomis 95650; 916-652-7252.

Festa Italiana (Sacramento)

Italian Cultural Society, P.O. Box 189427, Sacramento 95818; 916-ITALY-00; fax 916-ITALY-09.

Festival of Goat Cheese & North Coast Wine (Sonoma County)

Festival of Goat Cheese & North Coast Wine, 27955 King Ridge Road, Cazadero 95421; 707-847-3397; fax 707-823-6976.

Fish Feed & Art Festival (Trinidad)

Trinidad Chamber of Commerce, P.O. Box 356, Trinidad 95570; 707-677-0591.

Garlic Festival (Gilroy)

Gilroy Garlic Festival Association, Incorporated, P.O. Box 2311, 7473 Monterey Street, Gilroy 95021, 408-842-1625.

Gilroy Visitors Bureau, 7780 Monterey Street, Gilroy 95021, 408-842-6436; fax 408-842-6438.

Grape Stomp (Murphys)

Calaveras Wine Association, P.O. Box 2492, Murphys 95247; 209-795-5000.

Calaveras County Visitor Center, 1211 South Main Street, Angels Camp 95222; 800-225-3764 or 209-736-0049.

Grecian Festival (Novato)

Marin Grecian Festival, 1110 Dickson Drive, Novato 94949; 415-883-1998.

Historic Christmas Bed & Breakfast Tour (Calaveras County)

Calaveras County Visitor Center, P.O. Box 637, 1211 South Main Street, Angels Camp 95222; 800-225-3764 or 209-736-0049.

Italian Festa (Oakland)

Italian Festa, 77 Jack London Square, Suite L, Oakland 94607; 510-208-4646.

Oakland Convention & Visitors Bureau, 1000 Broadway, Suite 200, Oakland 94607; 800-2-OAKLAND or 510-839-9000; fax 510-839-9960.

Lambtown, U.S.A. Festival (Dixon)

Dixon District Chamber of Commerce, 201 South First Street, Dixon 95620; 916-678-2650.

Mid-Summer Scandinavian Festival (Ferndale)

Ferndale Chamber of Commerce, P.O. Box 325, Ferndale 95536; 707-786-4477.

Mountain Harvest Festival/A Taste of Quincy (Quincy)

Quincy Main Street Chamber, P.O. Box 3829, 372 W. Main Street, Suite 4, Quincy 95971; 916-283-0188.

Plumas County Visitors Bureau, P.O. Box 4120, 91 Church Street, Quincy 95971; 800-326-2247 or 916-283-6345; fax 916-283-5465.

Mushroom Mardi Gras (Morgan Hill)

Morgan Hill Chamber of Commerce, P.O. Box 786, 25 West First Street, Morgan Hill 95037; 408-779-9444; fax 408-779-6798.

Mustard Festival (Napa Valley)

Napa Valley Conference & Visitor's Bureau, 1310 Napa Town Center, Napa 94559; 707-226-7459; fax 707-255-2066.

Onion Festival (Vacaville)

Vacaville Onion Festival, Inc., P.O. Box 5263, Vacaville 95696; 707-448-4613; fax 707-448-4630.

Oyster Festival (Arcata)

Arcata Chamber of Commerce, 1062 G Street, Arcata 95521; 707-822-3619.

Pear Fair (Courtland)

Courtland Delta Pear Fair, P.O. Box 492, Courtland 95615; 916-775-1053.

California Delta Chambers, P.O. Box 177, 49 Main Street, Isleton 95641; 916-777-5007.

Pear Festival (Kelseyville)

Lake County Visitor Information Center, 875 Lakeport Boulevard, Lakeport 95453; 800-525-3743 or 707-263-9544; fax 707-263-9564.

Prune Festival (Yuba City)

California Prune Festival, P.O. Box 3006, Yuba City 95992; 916-671-3100.

Yuba-Sutter Chamber of Commerce, P.O. Box 1429, 10th & E Streets, Marysville 95901; 916-743-6501; fax 916-741-8645.

Pumpkin-Fest (Healdsburg)

Healdsburg Area Chamber of Commerce, 217 Healdsburg Avenue, Healdsburg 95448; 800-648-9922 or 707-433-6935.

Salmon Festival (Klamath)

Yurok Tribal Offices, 15900 Highway 101 North, Klamath 95548; 707-482-2921; fax 707-482-9465.

Klamath Chamber of Commerce, P.O. Box 476, Klamath, CA 95548; 707-482-5591.

Seafood, Art & Wine Festival (Bodega Bay)

Bodega Bay Area Chamber of Commerce, P.O. Box 146, 850 Highway 1, Bodega Bay 94923; 707-875-3422.

Snowfest! (Lake Tahoe)

Snowfest!, P.O. Box 7590, Tahoe City 96145; 916-563-7625; fax 916-583-8145.

Tahoe North Chamber of Commerce, P.O. Box 884, Tahoe City 96145; 916-581-6900.

Solar Cook-Off (Taylorsville)

Blackhawk Solar Access, P.O. Box 1468, Quincy 95971; 916-283-1396.

Plumas County Visitors Bureau, P.O. Box 4120, 91 Church Street, Quincy 95971; 800-326-2247 or 916-283-6345; fax 916-283-5465.

Timberfest (Sierra County)

Sierra County Chamber of Commerce, P.O. Box 206, Loyalton 96118; 800-200-4949 or 916-993-6900.

Walnut Festival (Walnut Creek)

Walnut Festival Association, P.O. Box 3408, Walnut Creek 94598; 510-935-6766; fax 510-935-7999.

Whale Festival (Fort Bragg)

Fort Bragg-Mendocino Coast Chamber of Commerce, P.O. Box 1141, Fort Bragg 95437; 800-726-2780 or 707-961-6300; fax 707-964-2056.

Zucchini Festival (Angels Camp)

Calaveras County Visitor Center, P.O. Box 637, 1211 South Main Street, Angels Camp 95222; 800-225-3764 or 209-736-0049.

INDEX

A

Abalone
  Abalone Traditional 13
  Garlic Abalone Noodles 11
  Thai Abalone Hors d'Oeuvres 12
Abalone Dive 9
Abalone Traditional 13
Albacore
  Grilled Albacore Steaks 168
An Elegant Victorian Mansion Bed & Breakfast
      Inn 60, 61, 83
Anderson Marsh State Historic Park 37
Angels Camp 196
Anise and Bodega Goat Cheese on Baby Bok
      Choy 80
Appetizers
  Anise and Bodega Goat Cheese on Baby Bok
      Choy 80
  Artichoke Dip 103
  Aspara-kopitas 29
  Barbecued Walnuts 189
  California Swordfish Ceviche 170
  Crab and Brie Loaf 169
  Danish Meat Balls 118
  Dolomathes Yialandji 97
  Eggplant Antipasta 90
  Grilled Herb Encrusted Chicken 121
  Linda's Salmon Party Log 164
  Marinated Mushrooms 102
  Oyster with Spinach Pesto 142
  Patè de Foies de Volaille 60
  Pearl Onions in Raspberry Wine Vinegar
      Sauce 135
  Ricotta, Prosciutto and Basil Spread 106
  Savory Walnut Snacks 191
  Smoked Salmon Mousse 83
  Snappy Bean Dip 67
  Spicy Yam Cakes 104
  Thai Abalone Hors d'Oeuvres 12
  Tiropetes 99
  Vegitaters 122
  Xim Xim Eggplant 72
Apples
  Blackberry and Apple Crumble a la Mode 38
  Blackberry Preserves 40
  Roast Pork with Brandied Apples 36

Apricot Piña Colada 15
Apricots
  Apricot Piña Colada 15
  Chinese Apricot Chicken 16
  Dried Apricot-Pistachio Biscotti 18
  Stir-Fry Pork and Apricots 17
  Whole Grain Apricot Mustard 132
Arcata 138
Artichoke Dip 103
Artichokes
  Artichoke Dip 103
Aspara-kopitas 29
Asparagus
  Aspara-kopitas 29
  Asparagus Lasagna 32
  Asparagus Poppy Seed Loaf 31
  Cold and Spicy Mushroom Noodles 126
  San Joaquin Valley Enchiladas 30
Asparagus Lasagna 32
Asparagus Poppy Seed Loaf 31
Avery Hotel 100
Avocado
  Salmon with Avocado Cream Sauce 22

B

Baked Pears 147
Baked Stuffed Onion Enchiladas 137
Banana Fluff 181
Bananas
  Banana Fluff 181
Barbecue Chicken Kabobs 21
Barbecued Walnuts 189
Beans
  Beefy Baked Beans 42
  Brazilian Black Bean Soup 178
  Brownie's Sweet Venison Chili 47
  Chili Beans 48
  Limas con Chile y Queso 65
  Plantation Blackeyes 66
  Portuguese-Style Bean Soup 68
  Snappy Bean Dip 67
  White Bean Soup 179
Bear
  Bear Roast 175
Bear Roast 175

Beef
  Beefy Baked Beans 42
  Chili Beans 48
  Danish Meat Balls 118
  Grilled California Short Ribs 186
  Marinated Chuck Roast 93
  Pumpkin Soup 160
  Spicy California Chili 49
  Tuxedo Mushroom Burgers 127
Beefy Baked Beans 42
Best Restaurant Boston Clam Chowder 57
Best Restaurant Manhattan Chowder 56
Better'n Mom's Prune Cake 156
Betty Jayne's Garlic Soup with Cheese Bread
      89
Beverages
  Apricot Piña Colada 15
Birria de Borrego 114
Blackberries
  Blackberries 'n' Cream 39
  Blackberry and Apple Crumble a la Mode 38
  Blackberry Preserves 40
Blackberries 'n' Cream 39
Blackberry and Apple Crumble a la Mode 38
Blackberry Preserves 40
Bo-Cah Ama Council 9
Boccie Ball 107
Bodega Bay 167
Brazilian Black Bean Soup 178
Breads
  Asparagus Poppy Seed Loaf 31
  Choco-light Muffins 51
  Cranberry-Orange Muffins 63
  Focaccia 4, 101
  Quick Pear Bread 145
  Swedish Rye Bread 117
  Swiss Scones 61
  Zucchini Pancakes 197
Broiled Pacific Salmon with Tapenade of
      Calamata Olives, Sun-dried Tomato, and
      Leek, Served with Chef's Compound
      Butter 131
Brownie's Sweet Venison Chili 47
Butter
  Chef's Compound Butter 131
  Garlic Butter 88

C

Calaveras County 100
California Cioppino 85
California Department of Fish and Game 9
California Salmon Quiche 165
California Salmon Tostadas 166
California Swordfish Ceviche 170
Cheesecake 180
Cheeses
    Anise and Bodega Goat Cheese on Baby Bok
        Choy 80
    Crab and Brie Loaf 169
    Duck and Walnut Enchiladas 20
    Fromage Blanc with Caramelized Onions 8
    Grilled Polenta with Sonoma Jack Cheese
        23
    Grilled Smoked Turkey with Chevre Cheddar
        on Black 81
    Parmesan Glazed Halibut Fillets 123
    Pears, Port and Stilton Cheese 151
    Ricotta, Prosciutto and Basil Spread 106
    Ricotta Sfingi 75
    Tiropetes 99
Chef Sal's Manhattan-Style Clam Chowder 58
Chef's Compound Butter 131
Cherries
    Beefy Baked Beans 42
    Cherry and Wine Sauce 45
    Cherry Delicious Ribs 184
    Grilled Duck Breast with Cherry Sauce 94
    No-Bake Cherry Cheese Squares 43
    Sweet Cherry Sauce in Meringue Shells 44
Cherry and Wine Sauce 45
Cherry Delicious Ribs 184
Chicken. See Poultry
Chicken Breasts with Walnut Orange Sauce
    190
Chili
    Brownie's Sweet Venison Chili 47
    Chili Beans 48
    Spicy California Chili 49
Chili Beans 48
Chili Peppers
    Birria de Borrego 114
    Jalapeño Relleno 79
China Flat Museum 46
Chinese Apricot Chicken 16
Choco-light Muffins 51
Chocolate
    Choco-light Muffins 51
    Chocolate Chip Pumpkin Loaf 26
    Deep Dark Chocolate Cake 54

Hershey's Cocoa Cream Pie 52
    White Chocolate-Fig Pie 53
Chocolate Chip Pumpkin Loaf 26
Christmas Favorite Coconut-Pecan Bars 62
Clams
    Best Restaurant Boston Clam Chowder 57
    Best Restaurant Manhattan Chowder 56
    Chef Sal's Manhattan-Style Clam Chowder
        58
    Grilled Oysters and Clams with Spicy Cajun
        Sauce 139
Cold and Spicy Mushroom Noodles 126
Concours d'Elegance 28
Condiments
    Spicy Grapes 133
    Warm Peach-Mustard Compote 130
Cookies
    Dried Apricot-Pistachio Biscotti 18
    Pear-Pistachio Fruit Chews 149
    Sprut Cookies 116
Cooper House Bed & Breakfast Inn 100
Coq au Vin 2
Courtland 143
Courtyard Bed & Breakfast Inn 100
Couscous
    Prune Couscous 155
Crab
    Crab and Brie Loaf 169
    Lake Tahoe Crab Cakes 172
    Murphys Hotel Crab Cakes 105
Crab and Brie Loaf 169
Crackers, Spiced 8
Cranberries
    Cranberry-Orange Muffins 63
Cranberry-Orange Muffins 63
Cucumbers
    Danish Cucumber Salad 119

D

Danish Cucumber Salad 119
Danish Meat Balls 118
Deep Dark Chocolate Cake 54
Desserts
    Asparagus Poppy Seed Loaf 31
    Baked Pears 147
    Banana Fluff 181
    Better'n Mom's Prune Cake 156
    Blackberries 'n' Cream 39
    Blackberry and Apple Crumble a la Mode 38
    Cheesecake 180
    Chocolate Chip Pumpkin Loaf 26
    Christmas Favorite Coconut-Pecan Bars 62

Deep Dark Chocolate Cake 54
    Eggplant Strudel 70
    Hershey's Cocoa Cream Pie 52
    My Nutty Pumpkin Pie 158
    No-Bake Cherry Cheese Squares 43
    Pear Cobbler 144
    Pears, Port and Stilton Cheese 151
    Pumpkin Cake Roll 25
    Ricotta Sfingi 75
    Sinless Pumpkin Pie 159
    Snow Ice Cream 173
    Sweet Cherry Sauce in Meringue Shells 44
    White Chocolate-Fig Pie 53
    Zucchini Cake 200
Dixon 112
Dolomathes Yialandji 97
Dorrington Hotel 100
Dried Apricot-Pistachio Biscotti 18
Duck. See Poultry
Duck and Walnut Enchiladas with Tomatillo
    Sauce an 20
Dunbar House Bed & Breakfast Inn 100

E

Easy Eggplant Parmesan 73
Eggplant
    Easy Eggplant Parmesan 73
    Eggplant Antipasta 90
    Eggplant Strudel 70
    New Loomis Eggplant Salad 71
    Xim Xim Eggplant 72
Eggplant Antipasta 90
Eggplant Strudel 70
Eggs
    California Salmon Quiche 165
    Surimi Seafood-Zucchini Frittata with Fresh
        Tomato 84
Enchiladas
    Baked Stuffed Onion Enchiladas 137
    Duck and Walnut with Tomatillo Sauce 20
    San Joaquin Valley Enchiladas 30
Exquisite Pear and Spinach Salad 152

F

Ferndale 115
Fig and Sun-dried Tomato Pizza 109
Figs
    Fig and Sun-dried Tomato Pizza 109
    White Chocolate-Fig Pie 53
Fillet of Pork with Prune Sauce 154
Firemans' Muster 14

Flounder
    Flounder Fillets Dijon 195
Flounder Fillets Dijon 195
Focaccia 4, 101
Fort Bragg 192
Forty-Clove Chicken Filice 87
Fresh Tuna Salad Nicoise 7
Fromage Blanc with Caramelized Onions 8

G

Garlic
    Betty Jayne's Garlic Soup with Cheese
      Bread 89
    Eggplant Antipasta 90
    Forty-Clove Chicken Filice 87
    Garlic Abalone Noodles 11
    Garlic Butter 88
Garlic Abalone Noodles 11
Garlic Butter 88
Gilroy 86
Ginger Wasabi Mustard 132
Gnocchi di Patate 110
Grape Leaves
    Dolomathes Yialandji 97
Grapes
    Sautéed Pork Medallions with Whole Grain
      Mustard and Spicy Grapes 133
    Spicy Grapes 133
Great Chowder Chase 55
Grilled Albacore Steaks 168
Grilled California Short Ribs 186
Grilled Duck Breast with Cherry Sauce 94
Grilled Herb Encrusted Chicken 121
Grilled Oysters and Clams with Spicy Cajun
    Sauce 139
Grilled Polenta with Sonoma Jack Cheese 23
Grilled Smoked Turkey with Chevre Cheddar on
    Black 81
Guacamole 166

H

Half Moon Bay 24
Halibut
    Parmesan Glazed Halibut Fillets 123
Healdsburg 157
Heather Farm Park 187
Hershey Plant Tours 50
Hershey's Cocoa Cream Pie 52
Honey Dijon Mustard 132
Horseshoe Tournament 14
Hot Air Ballooning 14, 128
Humboldt County 59

I

Italian Zucchini Bake 198

J

Jack London Square 107
Jalapeño Relleno 79

K

Kelseyville 148
Klamath 162

L

Lake County 37
Lake Tahoe 171
Lake Tahoe Crab Cakes 172
Lamb
    Birria de Borrego 114
    Roast Loin of Lamb 95
    Souvlaki 98
    Uncle Ernie's Stuffed Leg of Lamb 113
Lasagna ala Ferrarese 3
Limas con Chile y Queso 65
Linda's Salmon Party Log 164
Linguini Pescatore 108
Liver
    Patè de Foies de Volaille 60
Lodge at Manuel Mill 100
Lodi 41
Logger & Cowboy Poetry and Music Show 182
Logging Contests 162, 182
Loomis 69
Loyalton 183

M

Mammoth Creek Park 19
Mammoth Lakes 19
Marin Ballet 1
Marin County 1
Marin Opera 1
Marin Symphony 1
Marinated Chuck Roast 93
Marinated Mushrooms 102
Meats
    Bear Roast 175
    Beefy Baked Beans 42
    Birria de Borrego 114
    Brazilian Black Bean Soup 178
    Brownie's Sweet Venison Chili 47
    Cherry Delicious Ribs 184
    Chili Beans 48
    Danish Meat Balls 118
    Fillet of Pork with Prune Sauce 154
    Grilled California Short Ribs 186
    Lasagna ala Ferrarese 3
    Marinated Chuck Roast 93
    Pear-Pork Wild Rice Salad 150
    Penne al Salami 76
    Pumpkin Soup 160
    Roast Loin of Lamb 95
    Roast Pork with Brandied Apples 36
    Sautéed Pork Medallions with Whole Grain
      Mustard a 133
    Souvlaki 98
    Spicy California Chili 49
    Stir-Fry Pork and Apricots 17
    Sweet and Sour Pork Ribs 185
    Tuxedo Mushroom Burgers 127
    Uncle Ernie's Stuffed Leg of Lamb 113
    Venison Chops 174
Mendocino 9–10
Micke Grove Regional Park 41
Mixed Grill of Seafoods 132
Morgan Hill 124
Murphys 91
Murphys Historic Hotel & Lodge 100
Murphys Hotel Crab Cakes 105
Mushroom Garden Baked Potatoes 125
Mushrooms
    Cold and Spicy Mushroom Noodles 126
    Marinated 102
    Mushroom Garden Baked Potatoes 125
    Sauvignon Mushrooms 92
    Tuxedo Mushroom Burgers 127
    Wild Mushroom Pizza with Polenta Fennel
      Crust 35
Mustard
    Ginger Wasabi Mustard 132
    Honey Dijon Mustard 132
    Vinaigrette 152
    Whole Grain Apricot Mustard 132
My Nutty Pumpkin Pie 158

N

Nativity of Christ Greek Orthodox Church 96
New Loomis Eggplant Salad 71
No-Bake Cherry Cheese Squares 43
Novato 96

O

Oak Grove Regional Park 28
Oakdale 50
Oakland 107
Onions
    Baked Stuffed Onion Enchiladas 137
    Fromage Blanc with Caramelized Onions 8
    Pearl Onions in Raspberry Wine Vinegar
        Sauce 135
    Voracious Vacaville Burgers 136
Oranges
    Chicken Breasts with Walnut Orange Sauce
        190
    Pumpkin Orange Oyster Bisque 141
Oyster with Spinach Pesto 142
Oysters
    Grilled Oysters and Clams with Spicy Cajun
        Sauce 139
    Oyster with Spinach Pesto 142
    Oysters Rockefeller Pizza 140
    Pumpkin Orange Oyster Bisque 141
Oysters Rockefeller Pizza 140

P

Paella Valenciana 6
Parmesan Glazed Halibut Fillets 123
Pasta
    Asparagus Lasagna 32
    Cold and Spicy Mushroom Noodles 126
    Gnocchi di Patate 110
    Lasagna ala Ferrarese 3
    Linguini Pescatore 108
    Penne al Salami 76
    Savory Spaghetti Sauce 77
Patè de Foies de Volaille 60
Patterson 14
Peaches
    Warm Peach-Mustard Compote 130
Pear Cobbler 144
Pear-Pistachio Fruit Chews 149
Pear-Pork Wild Rice Salad 150
Pear-Raspberry Jam 146
Pearl Onions in Raspberry Wine Vinegar Sauce
    135
Pears
    Baked Pears 147
    Exquisite Pear and Spinach Salad 152
    Pear Cobbler 144
    Pear-Pistachio Fruit Chews 149
    Pear-Pork Wild Rice Salad 150
    Pear-Raspberry Jam 146

Pears, Port and Stilton Cheese 151
    Quick Pear Bread 145
Pears, Port and Stilton Cheese 151
Pecans
    Christmas Favorite Coconut-Pecan Bars 62
Penne al Salami 76
Pickled Pumpkin 27
Pistachios
    Dried Apricot-Pistachio Biscotti 18
    Pear-Pistachio Fruit Chews 149
Pizza
    Fig and Sun-dried Tomato Pizza 109
    Oysters Rockefeller Pizza 140
    Wild Mushroom Pizza with Polenta Fennel
        Crust 35
Plantation Blackeyes 66
Polenta
    Grilled Polenta with Sonoma Jack Cheese
        23
    Polenta Fennel Pizza Crust 35
Pork
    Cherry Delicious Ribs 184
    Danish Meat Balls 118
    Fillet of Pork with Prune Sauce 154
    Pear-Pork Wild Rice Salad 150
    Ricotta, Prosciutto and Basil Spread 106
    Roast Pork with Brandied Apples 36
    Sautéed Pork Medallions with Whole Grain
        Mustard and Spicy Grapes 133
    Stir-Fry Pork and Apricots 17
    Sweet and Sour Pork Ribs 185
Portuguese-Style Bean Soup 68
Potatoes
    Gnocchi di Patate 110
    Mushroom Garden Baked Potatoes 125
    Vegitaters 122
    Whole-Grain Mustard Potato Salad 129
Poultry
    Baked Stuffed Onion Enchiladas 137
    Barbecue Chicken Kabobs 21
    Chicken Breasts with Walnut Orange Sauce
        190
    Chinese Apricot Chicken 16
    Coq au Vin 2
    Duck and Walnut Enchiladas with Tomatillo
        Sauce an 20
    Forty-Clove Chicken Filice 87
    Grilled Duck Breast with Cherry Sauce 94
    Grilled Herb Encrusted Chicken 121
    Grilled Smoked Turkey with Chevre Cheddar
        on Black Bread 81
    Paella Valenciana 6
    San Joaquin Valley Enchiladas 30
    Turkey Breast Fillets ala Marsala 111

Preserves
    Blackberry 40
    Pear-Raspberry Jam 146
Prune Couscous 155
Prunes
    Better'n Mom's Prune Cake 156
    Fillet of Pork with Prune Sauce 154
    Prune Couscous 155
Pumpkin
    Chocolate Chip Pumpkin Loaf 26
    My Nutty Pumpkin Pie 158
    Pickled Pumpkin 27
    Pumpkin Cake Roll 25
    Pumpkin Fest Stew 161
    Pumpkin Orange Oyster Bisque 141
    Pumpkin Soup 160
    Sinless Pumpkin Pie 159
Pumpkin Cake Roll 25
Pumpkin Fest Stew 161
Pumpkin Orange Oyster Bisque 141
Pumpkin Soup 160

Q

Quick Pear Bread 145
Quilt show 148
Quincy 120

R

Raspberries
    Pear-Raspberry Jam 146
Redbud Inn 100
Redwood Dairy Goat Association 78
Rice
    Paella Valenciana 6
    Pear-Pork Wild Rice Salad 150
    Pilaf 98
Ricotta, Prosciutto and Basil Spread 106
Ricotta Sfingi 75
Roast Loin of Lamb 95
Roast Pork with Brandied Apples 36
Roasted Miwok Salmon 34

S

Sacramento 74
Salads
    Anise and Bodega Goat Cheese on Baby Bok
        Choy 80
    Danish Cucumber Salad 119
    Exquisite Pear and Spinach Salad 152
    Fresh Tuna Salad Nicoise 7

New Loomis Eggplant Salad 71
Pear-Pork Wild Rice Salad 150
Whole-Grain Mustard Potato Salad 129
Salami
    Penne al Salami 76
Salmon
    Broiled Pacific Salmon with Tapenade of
        Calamata 0 131
    California Salmon Quiche 165
    California Salmon Tostadas 166
    Linda's Salmon Party Log 164
    Roasted Miwok Salmon 34
    Smoked Salmon Mousse 83
    with Avocado Cream Sauce 22
    Yurok-Style Barbecued Salmon 163
Salmon with Avocado Cream Sauce 22
San Francisco 5
San Joaquin Valley Enchiladas 30
San Rafael 1
Santa Cruz 55
Sauces
    Avocado Cream 22
    Barbecue 21
    Cherry 94
    Cherry and Wine 45
    Coconut Curry 12
    Peanut 12
    Prune 154
    Sauvignon Mushrooms 92
    Savory Spaghetti 77
    Spicy Cajun 139
    Tarator 188
    Tomatillo 20
Sautéed Pork Medallions with Whole Grain
    Mustard a 133
Sauvignon Mushrooms 92
Savory Spaghetti Sauce 77
Savory Walnut Snacks 191
Seafood
    Abalone Traditional 13
    Best Restaurant Boston Clam Chowder 57
    Best Restaurant Manhattan Chowder 56
    Broiled Pacific Salmon with Tapenade of
        Calamata 0 131
    California Cioppino 85
    California Salmon Quiche 165
    California Salmon Tostadas 166
    California Swordfish Ceviche 170
    Chef Sal's Manhattan-Style Clam Chowder
        58
    Crab and Brie Loaf 169
    Flounder Fillets Dijon 195
    Fresh Tuna Salad Nicoise 7
    Garlic Abalone Noodles 11

Grilled Albacore Steaks 168
Grilled Oysters and Clams with Spicy Cajun
    Sauce 139
Lake Tahoe Crab Cakes 172
Linda's Salmon Party Log 164
Linguini Pescatore 108
Mixed Grill of Seafoods 132
Murphys Hotel Crab Cakes 105
Paella Valenciana 6
Parmesan Glazed Halibut Fillets 123
Roasted Miwok Salmon 34
Salmon with Avocado Cream Sauce 22
Seafood Chowder 194
Seafood Red Chowder 193
Smoked Salmon Mousse 83
Surimi Seafood-Zucchini Frittata with Fresh
    Tomato 84
Thai Abalone Hors d'Oeuvres 12
Yurok-Style Barbecued Salmon 163
Seafood Chowder 194
Seafood Red Chowder 193
Sierra County 182–183
Sinless Pumpkin Pie 159
Smoked Salmon Mousse 83
Snappy Bean Dip 67
Snow Ice Cream 173
Solar Cooking 176
Sonoma County 78
Soups
    Best Restaurant Boston Clam Chowder 57
    Best Restaurant Manhattan Chowder 56
    Betty Jayne's Garlic Soup with Cheese
        Bread 89
    Brazilian Black Bean Soup 178
    Chef Sal's Manhattan-Style Clam Chowder
        58
    Portuguese-Style Bean Soup 68
    Pumpkin Orange Oyster Bisque 141
    Pumpkin Soup 160
    Seafood Chowder 194
    Seafood Red Chowder 193
    White Bean Soup 179
Souvlaki 98
Spicy California Chili 49
Spicy Yam Cakes 104
Spinach
    Exquisite Pear and Spinach Salad 152
    Spinach Pesto 142
Spinach Pesto 142
Sprut Cookies 116
Squaw Valley 33
Stews
    California Cioppino 85
    Coq Au Vin 2

Pumpkin Fest Stew 161
Stir-Fry Pork and Apricots 17
Stockton 28
Surimi Seafood-Zucchini Frittata with Fresh
    Tomato 84
Swedish Rye Bread 117
Sweet and Sour Pork Ribs 185
Sweet Cherry Sauce in Meringue Shells 44
Swiss Scones 61
Swordfish
    California Swordfish Ceviche 170

T

Tarator Sauce 188
Taylorsville 176–177
Thai Abalone Hors d'Oeuvres 12
Tiropetes 99
Tomatillos
    Duck and Walnut Enchiladas with Tomatillo
        Sauce an 20
Tomatoes
    Fig and Sun-dried Tomato Pizza 109
    Zucchini Tomato Casserole 199
Tracy 64
Trinidad 82
Trinidad Head Lighthouse Tour 82
Truckee 171
Tuna
    Fresh Tuna Salad Nicoise 7
Turkey. See Poultry
Turkey Breast Fillets ala Marsala 111
Tuxedo Mushroom Burgers 127

U

Uncle Ernie's Stuffed Leg of Lamb 113
Utica Park 196

V

Vacaville 134
Van Damme State Park 10
Vegitaters 122
Venison
    Brownie's Sweet Venison Chili 47
    Venison Chops 174
Venison Chops 174
Voracious Vacaville Burgers 136

W

Walnut Creek 187

Walnuts
    Barbecued 189
    Chicken Breasts with Walnut Orange Sauce
        190
    Duck and Walnut Enchiladas with Tomatillo
        Sauce an 20
    Savory Walnut Snacks 191
    Tarator Sauce 188
Warm Peach-Mustard Compote 130
Whale Watching 192
White Bean Soup 179
White Chocolate-Fig Pie 53
Whole Grain Apricot Mustard 132
Whole Grain Mustard Potato Salad 129
Wild Game & Fish Cook-off 171
Wild Mushroom Pizza with Polenta Fennel Crust
    35
Willow Creek 46

X

Xim Xim Eggplant 72

Y

Yams
    Spicy Yam Cakes 104
Yellow Dog Inn 100
Yellow Ribbon Rally 182
Youth in Arts 1
Yuba City 153
Yurok Indian Tribe 162
Yurok-Style Barbecued Salmon 163

Z

Zucchini
    Italian Zucchini Bake 198
    Surimi Seafood-Zucchini Frittata with Fresh
        Tomato 84
    Zucchini Cake 200
    Zucchini Pancakes 197
    Zucchini Tomato Casserole 199
Zucchini Cake 200
Zucchini Pancakes 197
Zucchini Tomato Casserole 199

ABOUT THE AUTHOR

Bob Carter is an award-winning travel writer and columnist. He has served on the faculty of Pasadena City College; California State University, Los Angeles; and the University of Oregon. He received a 1993 "Best of Series of Short Stories" award from the Outdoor Writers Association of California. He is an active member of the International Food, Wine, & Travel Writers Association and Outdoor Writers Association of California. His ongoing travel columns appear in a variety of newpapers and magazines. He is author of the popular travel book, *The Best of Central California: Main Roads & Side Trips*. When not traveling, he resides in the coastal community of Oxnard, California.